Surviving the Second Civil War

The Land Rights Battle . . . and How To Win It

Timothy Robert Walters

RAWHIDE
WESTERN
PUBLISHING

Safford, Arizona

First Edition: Published by Rawhide Western Publishing
Cover design by Renee Anthony Agency

Typeset in Times New Roman on Intel computers by Rawhide Western
Publishing, P.O Box 327, Safford, Arizona 85548.
Telephone 602-428-5956. Fax 602-428-7010.

Printed in the United States of America . . . the Land of Freedom and
Inalienable Rights.

Walters, Timothy Robert, 1945
        Surviving the second civil war : the land rights battle . . .
        and how to win it
America / Timothy Robert Walters. — 1st ed.

        Includes bibliographical references and index.

        ISBN 0-9641935-0-7 : $12.95

        Library of Congress Catalog Card Number : 94-66993
                                                        CIP

Surviving the Second Civil War

Other books by Timothy Robert Walters:

Judevar (western fiction)

ACKNOWLEDGMENTS

In an effort such as this there are always more grateful acknowledgments for more reasons than there are ways to repay the debts of gratitude. I extend my sincerest thanks to:

Danny Fryar . . . Reserve, New Mexico
Steve Emerine . . . Tucson, Arizona
John Ratje . . . Safford, Arizona
Carloss Bashista . . . Glenwood, New Mexico
Mark Herrington . . . Safford, Arizona
Steve Eady . . . Safford, Arizona
Little Leon Somerville . . . Cozahome, Arkansas
Joe Snyder . . . Pueblo, Colorado
Howard Hutchinson . . . Glenwood, New Mexico
Margaret Gabbard . . . Boise, Idaho
David Ridinger . . . Phoenix, Arizona
Leri Thomas . . . Wolftown, Virginia
Chester Sellman . . . Murphy, Idaho
Ben L. Smith . . . Safford, Arizona
Barbara Jayo . . . Murphy, Idaho
Wayne Hage . . . Tonopah, Nevada
Cliff Gardner . . . Ruby Valley, Nevada
Ann Corcoran . . . Sharpsburg, Maryland
Glen Dowdle . . . Safford, Arizona
Skelly Boyd . . . Safford, Arizona
Stanley Walters . . . Lakeview, Oregon
Joe Carter . . . Safford, Arizona
Dean Kleckner . . . Park Ridge, Illinois
Jeff Davis . . . Phoenix, Arizona
Don Sanborn . . . Lakeview, Oregon
Ben Smith . . . Eden, Arizona
Gilbert Esquerdo . . . Tucson, Arizona
Skip Cochran . . . Safford, Arizona
Rob Daniels . . . Tucson, Arizona
Don Sherwood . . . Denver, Colorado
Jean Reynolds . . . Sweet Home, Oregon
John Kunzman . . . Sweet Home, Oregon

Dedication:

*I pledge allegiance to the flag
of the United States of America,
and to the Republic for which it stands,
one nation under God, indivisible,
with liberty and justice for all.*

**In Memory of
Dixy Lee Ray
1914 - 1994**

CONTENTS

Bibliography

Index

FOREWORD

We live in a land of opportunity. The reason we are a prosperous people is because we respect our freedom and our Constitution. We try to limit the size of our government. We have a wonderful, strong, heartfelt belief in private property rights, and because of those things we are a prosperous people.

To say that property is the cornerstone of liberty comes up short. I would say that property *is* liberty. I believe that with all my heart and soul. You start fooling around with private property rights and you are on the road to slavery. The only thing left with any power at all would be a large central government.

The word "property" comes from a Latin word that means "ownership," and I would say that the concepts of ownership and proprietorship are "freedom." Apply those concepts to the human mind and spirit and you develop freedom of speech . . . and you develop freedom of worship. It all emanates from that. You apply them to the human person and you develop freedom to travel and the right of an accused to due process of law. You apply them to *land* and you develop the rights to have and enjoy private property, and that's what we are all about as *people*.

Each of us is born into life as a proprietor of a mind and of a body and, some of us would say, a soul, and I believe that. All human achievement depends upon our freedom to exercise that proprietorship and our diligence in exercising it with virtue and responsibility.

For anyone who doubts the importance or the power of private property, two things ought to be prescribed. First, take a look around the world during the closing decades of this 20th century. The crumbling Communist Bloc reduced to its most basic meaning is one grand affirmation of the power of private property. And second, just take a look around you here at home. Consider the greatness of this nation and its historical gift for generating capital and wealth. There has never been anything like it in the history of mankind. And from the beginning, these things have been built entirely on a foundation of private property rights. It's just that simple. That's where it begins and that's where it ends. That's the cradle of freedom.

I've always been fascinated by the inner-play between the government sector and the free enterprise system, and the broader implications in that struggle with regard to our economic liberty. And so it was a very interesting moment (in 1992) when the Arizona Legislature passed a bill to protect Fifth Amendment property rights. On the surface (it) seemed like a very simple little piece of legislation. I don't think it was identified on any of our lists as being a particularly incendiary bill. Its only real effect was to require the attorney general of this state to review Fifth Amendment "takings" law and draft guidelines based upon existing court decisions. Government was going to look before it leaped. Nothing in the bill proposed to create any new property rights beyond what the Supreme Court has already established. It was simply a device to require a state to consider Fifth Amendment rights *before* it imposed intended regulations rather than leaving the costly burden of legal actions on property owners.

We're adhered to our constitutional principles. I don't know how it got reversed in the first place. It never should have developed into what it has developed into—throwing people in prison who dug ponds years ago to water their cattle. Today, (those ponds) are "wetlands." (You) go to change it . . . the environmental police are there and (you) are prosecuted. That's not America, and we're not going to let it be America!

The controversy over this bill was absolutely amazing. I had agency heads and members of my own staff come into my office and say, "Governor, you can't sign that bill."

I said, "I'm supporting the Constitution of the United States of America. I believe in private property and I, therefore, believe in freedom. Why can't I sign that bill?"

"Well, it's just wrong because it's going to impede environmental progress."

"Well," I said, "if environmental progress means repealing the Constitution of the United States and doing away with private property rights, then my vote goes for private property."

There were key people on my staff—and a few agency heads—who said, "If you sign that bill, we are going to resign."

I got them all together and said, "I was elected Governor to defend the Constitution, and to uphold things like private property rights. Private property rights are a *civil* right. It's in the Constitution, and I'm going to sign the bill."

In the end, I signed the bill (and) nobody resigned.

The bill was labeled the "Polluter's Protection Act" by the state's second largest newspaper. Some of my own environmental people said my strong environmental record would be ruined. I don't believe my record has been ruined; I stand tall for the environment. But I will never impinge upon private property rights.

The environmental lobby has really kept up its pressure. They made the bill the subject of a desperate fundraising letter. They vilified me, and they have enough signatures to put this issue on the ballot in November of 1994. Arizona (will) conduct the first public vote in history on private property rights, and I think that is wonderful.

Once we settle this issue, we can start working to pass similar laws for local governments which impose a good deal more regulations affecting private property than state government. I think we should carry on this crusade.

Fife Symington
Governor of Arizona
—from an address before the 72nd annual meeting of the Arizona Farm Bureau, 1993

PREFACE

The "American Dream" is epitomized by the owning of land. America, from its birth, has been that wonderful free land where men and women could follow their hearts, decide what they wanted to do and be, set goals, educate themselves, roll up their sleeves and achieve successes through planning, hard work and perseverance.

It all hinged on owning a piece of land—nesting in a rich meadow, homesteading farms and ranches, staking mining claims. The resources were used to build cabins and whole cities. Farmers and ranchers supplied the food for a burgeoning populace. Prospectors found the materials to build railroads and machinery and communications systems. America was made great by Americans owning and working their lands.

A segment of contemporary society interprets all that activity and progress as a massive and brutal rape of the earth. Those pioneering settlers of the West and all the industrial entrepreneurs who followed are now viewed as thugs and villains who cared about nothing but their own prosperity. A movement is underway to restore North America to some vision of Eden that *must* have existed here before the first ships came.

The assault on property rights is coming from many fronts—politicians, federal agencies, regulation-obsessed bureaucrats, elite and well-funded preservationist groups, independent agencies with government approval, the federal government itself. Legislators are enacting hundreds of new laws based on the agendas of well-financed special interest groups, powerful federal bureaucrats and noetic idealists.

At stake are the fundamental civil liberties guaranteed in the U.S. Constitution and Bill of Rights. These founding principles, which provided the basis for establishing the strongest nation in the world, are being diluted and ignored.

The new wave of ill-conceived philosophy is threatening the very foundation of the American Dream. Farmers cannot work their own land. Ranchers are being regulated out of business. Miners can no longer explore the earth for minerals and metals. Entire towns are dying because of lost timber sales. Wetlands and endangered species and national parks and wild and scenic rivers are killing industry, freezing development and idling private land.

In the research processes for this book, a single call to the Farm Bureau Federation netted a box weighing *25 pounds*, filled with "horror stories" pertaining only to farmers and wetlands. There could be several books written from that one collection of farmers' personal stories. The picture is much broader than that, however.

The assaults are directed at private property owners and all the traditional users of federally managed lands. They are aimed at cultures and customs that have existed in this country longer than it's been a country. (Cattle grazing in New Mexico has been going on for 400 years.) The federal government is bound by its own law to *protect* established customs and cultures. Still, logging towns are dying, farmers are buying groceries with food stamps, and cowboys, prospectors and fishermen are not allowed to work.

In this book, we are going to take a hard look at the eroding American Dream. There will be stories of real people trapped in tangled webs of preposterous regulation, stuck in quagmires of bureaucratic red tape and suffocated in whirlpools of frivolous litigation. And just when you think this book is about *private* property rights, you'll find yourself reading about a war currently being waged over unappropriated lands rights and uses. But it's all about *rights*.

It's about losing your claim to America.

Is it too late to fight back, to make a stand for the preservation of the American way of life? Will the American public permit itself to be pressed into a system of feudalism?

I don't think so.

While this book will show you just how tenuous your hold is on so-called "inalienable rights," you will also meet some courageous "pioneers" of today who are fighting back in innovative and effective ways. And you will learn about methods to join in the battles. Together, we will examine ways of stemming the tide of aggression, of neutralizing the movement against personal rights and freedoms.

This book is not a text just for the farmer or rancher who has already experienced the effects of restrictive legislation, summary judgment, and the loss of crops and property. This book is for anyone who cares about the principles upon which our nation was founded. It's for those who are truly mindful of the environment and interested in a coexistence between nature and the human element. It's for impressionable young people who are absorbing a one-sided environmental curriculum in public schools. It's for anyone who lives in a house or rides in an automobile or eats food or wears clothing or likes to hunt or fish or sightsee or enjoys raising a garden or mowing a lawn.

It's for everyone who believes—as Thomas Jefferson did—that our Creator granted certain inalienable rights. It's for anyone who believes the U.S. Constitution is a good and workable blueprint for democracy.

This book is for anyone who loves America.

Timothy Robert Walters

INTRODUCTION

When undertaking a project such as this, a writer must establish a particular intent, or purpose. Then, with as much care and dignity (and passion) as possible, he or she must attempt to impart that intent, or purpose, to the reader without sermonizing.

My first impulse was to compile an enormous "horror story" on the subject of environmental overkill. However, I could see quickly that such a book would not serve my *purpose* because my *intent* was to *help* the reader more clearly perceive a very real danger and, in the end, offer some thoughts on what to do about it. As I said in the Preface, this entire book could be filled with outrageous stories based on wetlands determinations alone. But the picture is so much larger than that.

The erosion of property rights (and our constitutional guarantee of same) is so widespread today that it draws no distinction between classes or cultures. It has affected land developers, businessmen, farmers and ranchers, loggers and miners, and city-dwellers with lots barely as large as their homes. Michael Rowe, who is not allowed to add a room to his house in California, and Walt Disney Company, who cannot finish developing Disneyworld in Florida, are affected proportionately by the same loss of rights to the same bloated bureaucracies and radical preservation efforts.

Mark Herrington, a vice-president with the Arizona Farm Bureau, says it most poignantly: "If the state land department can come down . . . and confiscate my farm on the Gila River, they can have your house . . . "

He adds, "The basic fundamental principle of private property rights is the foundation of all rights, so if they can once trounce *anyone's* rights in private property, then there's no one protected."

Mark Pollot is an attorney in San Francisco who practices environmental and constitutional law. Formerly, he worked as a special assistant in the Land and Natural Resources Division of the U.S. Department of Justice. He wrote the "Takings Executive Order" in 1988. Those guidelines, signed by President Reagan, require the United States to consider the takings implication of its regulations.

Pollot knows the original intent has gone awry, and he says, "Regulations have become the government's means of circumventing the Fifth Amendment's 'just compensation' obligation. By not actually physically taking the property, but rendering it useless nonetheless, the government often leaves a property owner with only one right—the right to pay taxes."

My intent is to demonstrate how widespread this practice is. All facets of American society are affected.

I want the American public to know what's happening to their neighbors all across this nation—and some possible reasons why. I want my readers to feel the helplessness and despair of those who have been (and are being) victimized, and to know that we all are vulnerable.

I am going to share the stories of numerous American believers affected by "causes"—endangered species, rangeland reform, national park designations and more. The result is always the same: individual property owners (taxpaying families) are deprived of their means of sustenance (their rights) through excessive regulation by relentless bureaucrats.

Mark Herrington says it's not too late to turn things around, but it's going to take more than a few "meetings" of disgruntled farmers at the tailgate of a pickup. He adds, "All Americans have to be informed . . . to see these things . . . to know what's happening in people's lives. They need to be aware."

That is my intent.

The loss of property rights (basic personal rights) is not just a problem facing farmers who have been stricken with unfair wetlands designations. It is a problem affecting the entire makeup of our country—water rights and mining claims stripped away for the "public good," ranchers forced out of business by escalating grazing fees (a form of property tax), communities dying because wildlife management has idled local timber industries, poor families dragged from their homes to accommodate the creation of national parks, municipal water supplies threatened by endangered species.

Herrington says government regulation today is "overkill to the point of stupidity—total stupidity." He says, "Current regulation practices make honest men dishonest."

Can the eroding American Dream be restored?

Before we examine some efforts and methods aimed at doing so, I am going to expand on the reasons why this task should not be left "for someone else to do." Neither should it be a disjointed approach with isolated groups fighting singular battles. Every man, woman and child in America who stands to lose a single civil right as provided for in the Constitution of the United States belong together in a unified front. Only a welling voice from the silent majority can turn the tide of politics and bureaucracy sweeping us all toward a system of feudalism.

It can be done; it has been started. A great many more must join the cause. Therefore, before I talk about ways to preserve the American foundation, I intend to show you how precarious our hold on freedom really is.

I:

THE GREAT AMERICAN NIGHTMARE

I. Incident on the Roaring Fork River

Dennis and Nile Gerbaz are brothers working their privately owned ranch near Carbondale, Colorado. For nearly 70 years, they have lived in harmony with the land along the Roaring Fork River.

Their father believed in the Great American Dream. Very near the beginning of this century, he arrived in this country from Italy and began the pursuit of his own destiny. After laboring for more than a decade in the coal mines of Colorado and Montana, he went back to Italy to marry his childhood sweetheart and bring her to "the Land of Promise." Upon their return to Colorado, they bought a piece land and established the Gerbaz Ranch.

Nile Gerbaz was born there in 1923. Three years later, Dennis was born. The brothers spent their lives from childhood working and nurturing their land, raising crops and tending cattle. When their father died in 1961, the only thing that changed about the operation of the Gerbaz Ranch was the loss of one pair of hands to share the work. Dennis and Nile continued to raise their cattle and grow their potatoes, oats and barley. And they continued to work in unity with the land—the provider of their livelihoods—perpetuating a legacy begun by an immigrant from northern Italy who had carried with him a dream of freedom and prosperity in a new land.

The Roaring Fork River is an impressive work of nature, plunging out of the wooded Sawatch Range on a steep descent toward the Colorado River near Glenwood Springs. It's a wild and beautiful river, fed largely by the melting snows of the Rocky Mountains to the east. It runs so swiftly in some places that streambed boulders tumble along under its force, causing a dull "roaring" sound—hence, the name. The Roaring Fork provides life to the woods and fields along its banks. As is the case with most mountain rivers, it is also an unforgiving water course, bursting upon occasion from its banks and sweeping away much of all that lies in its path.

Such was the reason that an upstream neighbor of Nile and Dennis Gerbaz applied for a Corps of Engineers 404 permit to repair a damaged levee in 1984. The neighbor was granted the permit and his work on the upstream levee in effect diverted the river flow from its main channel to a small side channel.

In a very short time, about five acres of the Gerbaz Ranch were flooded due to the upstream diversion. Dennis and Nile asked for a permit to correct the problem. For unexplained reasons, the regulating agency denied a COE 404 permit to the Gerbazes. Additionally, it refused to visit the Gerbaz Ranch.

In the spring of 1985, the swollen Roaring Fork formed a dam of rocks, trees and debris where the river had been diverted into the side channel, preventing flood waters from spilling over into the old channel. Consequently, another fifteen acres of the Gerbaz Ranch became inundated, and about five feet of top soil were washed away from a two-acre section.

Two more requests for on-site inspections by the Corps of Engineers went unheeded. Finally, in desperation, the Gerbazes sought legal advice and learned that a clause in the Clean Water Act of 1977 would allow them to take action to prevent further flooding and destruction of their property. They removed the obstruction from the river, carefully reconstructed a levee that had been washed away, and returned the water flow to the channel it had occupied for decades.

Although the COE could not find its way to the Gerbaz Ranch for an on-site inspection of flood damage and the need for corrective maintenance, the Environmental Protection Agency had no trouble responding to the ranch and presenting the brothers with a summons to federal court because of their actions. Attached to their summons was a fine of $43,580,000.

That was the day the Gerbaz brothers' nightmare began. By 1990, they had spent more than $55,000 in legal fees and many hundreds of hours of valuable time defending themselves in federal court. In addition to legal costs, lost time and an unfathomable fine assessment, the Gerbazes were ordered to devise a "river modification plan" at a projected cost of about $150,000.

Dennis Gerbaz says the ranch is worth far less than it was (this on official appraisal reports), and salability of the property is negatively affected. Also, the ability of Dennis and Nile to effectively farm the land has been greatly impaired by the need to spend excessive amounts of time with attorneys, "expert witnesses," surveyors, appraisers, giving depositions and appearing in court.

As a footnote to all this, the Gerbazes reveal that a cousin, Larry Gerbaz, helped them repair their ranch, as well as a levee on his own property where the river had broken through, taking out fences and outbuildings before eating a channel to within 50 feet of his doorway. By early 1992, Larry Gerbaz was facing fines of more than $100,000,000 for these two alleged violations. (At the same time, the fines imposed against Nile and Dennis had risen to over $51,000,000 each.) Larry Gerbaz wrote in a letter to Don Sanborn of Lakeview, Oregon: "We were told in December (1991) that it might be two years before this thing ever gets to trial and by then our fines might pay the national debt— can you imagine that!"

Dennis Gerbaz says simply, "In both cases, we were merely trying to protect our properties from the ravages of flooding and erosion by an out-of-control river with no help from any federal agency."

William Perry Pendley, President and Chief Legal Officer of Mountain States Legal Foundation, says one thing is clear: "The government is trying to make an example out of Dennis and Nile Gerbaz."

Pendley says another matter is less clear—the government's exact position regarding the Gerbaz brothers. It refuses to tell them _why_ they were sued. Intimations are abundant—one, that the Roaring Fork River created an "artificial wetland" when it flooded, and that to "de-water" it required a permit; two, that rebuilding a 50-year-old levee limited the unspecified "reach of the river"; and still another, the brothers simply were supposed to get a permit for their work and they did not.

There is a law which allows people like the Gerbazes to do what they did. Pendley calls it "a well-crafted exception" under the Clean Water Act that ranchers and farmers have used carefully for years. He says bureaucrats don't like the exemption very much because it allows people to make decisions on their own property, based on need, common sense and practicality, without government control.

Pendley believes that power-hungry agency bureaucrats would like to get rid of this sensible clause in an important piece of much broader legislation without having to go to Congress to do it. He says, therefore, they are trying to frighten every property owner in America by declaring war on selected individuals like Dennis and Nile Gerbaz.

II. **A Scourge of Beavers and Bureaucrats**

Just before Christmas of 1989, Ruby Henderson received notification from the Soil Conservation Service that two portions of her farm near Bixby, Oklahoma, had been classified as wetlands. The determination was made solely within the SCS Field Office in Tulsa and sent to the 80-year-old widow by mail. District Conservationist Samuel Combs explained in his initial letter to Mrs. Henderson that if she did not agree with the determination, she was allowed 15 days to request a "reconsideration."

Ruby Henderson appealed the wetlands determination within the week. About 40 days later, she received a second letter from Samuel Combs. He wrote presumptuously that Mrs. Henderson's request for reconsideration was "based on the fact that you did not want any land designated wetlands on your farm." Seemingly as a token gesture, Mr. Combs ruled that one acre of the designated wetlands was *not* wetland "but we must uphold the Wetland decision made by me on the six acres . . . because of the soils and presence of hydrophytic vegetation."

(Remember, these determinations were made in an office in a distant city without the benefit of on-site inspection).

Mr. Combs then informed Mrs. Henderson that she had the standard 15-day period within which she might appeal this response to her first appeal, and she was referred to Area Conservationist LeRoy Tull of the Soil Conservation Service Area Office in Claremore, Oklahoma.

In a meticulously drafted explanation to Mr. Tull, Ruby pointed out that the disputed six acres had been in bermuda and fescue grasses for _the previous 30 years!_ She went on: " . . . we were able to keep it mowed and cattle grazed it until the last two years and then the beavers came and dammed up the drainage ditch and backed water up on this land. We pulled out several beaver dams winter before last. Then they moved on down the ditch on my neighbor's land and no one has been able to keep the dams broken and no one has trapped the beavers. Right now the beaver dam is just across the fence from my property line and it is a big dam."

(These beavers were not indigenous to this ditch; they had been introduced here by another government agency!)

Mrs. Henderson explained that water flowing in the ditch was drainage from a mile or two away, and offered to show the ditch and its origins of flow to Mr. Tull.

More than a month later, LeRoy Tull corresponded to Mrs. Henderson that he acknowledged the true reason for her appeal—that the area in question had been a pasture and that beavers had dammed a ditch, causing water to stand on the land. In his next sentence, however, he ignored the very issue he had acknowledged and issued a summary judgment: "We have reviewed the wetland decisions and find that we must concur with the wetland determination made by Sam Combs."

Tull further admonished the widow Henderson by reminding her that any effort to drain, fill or pump, or to plant a crop in the pasture would make her ineligible for USDA benefits. Then he generously allowed her _another_ 15 days to appeal _his_ decision to C. Budd Fountain, State Conservationist for the SCS in Stillwater, Oklahoma.

Ten days later, Ruby mailed a letter to C. Budd Fountain, restating the detailed information about bermuda, fescue, drainage and beavers. This time, she sent copies of her letter to U.S. Senator Don Nickles and Dennis Howard, lobbyist for the Oklahoma Farm Bureau.

Six weeks later, Mr. Fountain responded: " . . . we have completed additional field investigations and a review of previous findings at the field office and area office levels. After evaluating all available information, we find that we must concur with the wetland determination originally made by Sam Combs . . . "

After that, statements made by Mr. Fountain become ludicrous. He said he understood Mrs. Henderson's primary concern was that she could not "drain the area to increase pasture production" when, in fact, all Mrs. Henderson wished to do was to *reclaim* a pasture lost to inundation caused by beavers. He established that wetland designation on the farm was based on the occurrence of soil and plants "typically" found in wetlands. He then explained to Mrs. Henderson that this area of her farm "has one to two feet of standing water on it for long periods of time" (caused by the implantation of beavers).

The not-difficult-to-prove claim by Mrs. Henderson to both LeRoy Tull and Budd Fountain that this had been a bermuda and fescue pasture, both mowed and grazed, for the last 30 years was summarily ignored.

Budd Fountain graciously extended to Mrs. Henderson *still another* 15-day period during which she could appeal his findings to Mr. Wilson Scaling, Chief of the Soil Conservation Service in Washington, D.C.

Ruby Henderson says her once-beautiful bermuda pasture has now grown up in cattails and weeds. At age 80, she was still managing her Oklahoma farm, mowing other pastures and overseeing the baling of her hay, as well as picking pecans. After a two-year dispute, nothing was any more resolved than when she received her first notice of wetlands determination from Sam Combs. Mrs. Henderson says the battle has cost her nothing in legal fees because she personally pursued the filing of appeals, but the process has cost a great deal in unneeded "worries."

In too many cases to be coincidental, the Agricultural Stabilization and Conservation Service (ASCS) and SCS seem to establish wetland determinations on language in the Food Security Act that was intended to *protect* landowners. The law states clearly that the "swampbuster provisions" are meant to "discourage the draining and cultivation of wetland that is (this is the important part) *unsuitable for agricultural production in its natural state."*

Ruby Henderson's pasture *was* suitable for agricultural production in its *natural state*, and it had been used as such for 30 years.

Lynn Walton of Imlay City, Michigan, sites another outrageous example of the "tunnel-vision" approach used by SCS bureaucrats in applying the swampbuster clause. In this case, Walton bought a farm where about two acres had become wet due to a broken tile line. He wished to repair the line and resume farming. He was threatened with his farm program benefits if he did so. In its natural state, the two-acre "wetland" was suitable and had been used for agricultural production.

There are many hundreds of similar stories from Maine to California. The most common enforcement tool used to "scare" farmers, ranchers and other landowners into compliance with often improper wetlands determinations and subsequent appeals rulings is the threatened loss of USDA and other farm program benefits. Congress itself mandated this method of intimidation and punishment by providing that agencies could " . . . *deny all Federal farm program benefits—including, but not limited to, price supports, farm storage facility loans, crop insurance, disaster payments, and Farmers Home Administration loans—to farmers who drain, fill, clear, or otherwise destroy the natural characteristics of wetlands to produce program commodities* . . . "

Ruby Henderson did not necessarily wish to produce "program commodities," and still she was threatened with the loss of benefits. The agency bureaucrats have taken a piece of strong legislation (probably intended for a few hard-case violators) and are using it as a club over the head of every landowner who does not agree with their hasty and often slipshod designations.

There are dozens of documented cases where courageous private property owners have persisted in battling wetlands designations until government agencies were forced to rescind their original determinations. These "wetlands" were usually identified from aerial photographs showing "mysterious shadowing," or other unreliable information. The frightening thing is, these mistaken determinations will stand forever, costing millions of dollars in lost crops and property devaluation, if they are not challenged—and many of them stand anyway.

Tom Knutson of Vermillion, South Dakota, reveals the "improper determination" of one of his cornfields. He writes: " . . . we just came through one of the wettest springs on record. The corn has been cultivated and sprayed on time and shows no signs of moisture stress." Knutson explains that he's farmed the field for 12 years, and his landlord and the landlord's father for many years before that. No one has ever lost a crop due to excess moisture. Further, some of the designated areas on his farm were "high sandy ridges that burn out even on good high-moisture years." Knutson says an SCS official put a question mark beside those areas and made him "sign the form" anyway. He calls the entire incident "totally stupid."

And yet the SCS was totally serious in trying to claim a part of Tom Knutson's farm.

A spokesman for the Anderson Seed Farms in Forman, North Dakota, sums up the general frustration of most conscientious and sound-thinking farm owners in the country today: " . . . senators and congressmen should start listening to the people who are involved instead of the environmental extremists, Sierra Clubs, Audubon Society, Fish and Wildlife Service . . . (who) could care less if I can make a living farming . . . With farming as competitive as it is, we have to be able to improve our land and farm it as it should be farmed for the sake of the community and land in general."

III. **A Nevada Wetland that Never Was**

In June of 1989, Steve Lucas purchased a portion of the 101 Ranch at Paradise Valley, Nevada, planning to increase production on his acreage by raising grains and alfalfa. About 40 acres of a 67-acre area already was equipped with underground pipeline and irrigation risers in place since 1978. The parcel of land was leveled that same year. Farmers know that soils can rise or settle over the years, so Lucas wanted to again "level" the area and complete the installation of irrigation pipeline to replace open ditches and crude man-made diversions.

Lucas, knowing the cost of the project would be extensive, decided to apply for assistance under a cost-sharing program. At that time he learned he could not "improve or level" any part of the land due to an existing wetland designation.

He appealed.

Walter Lamb, District Conservationist for the Winnemucca SCS, and some other "experts" came to the 101 Ranch and determined that the soil hydrology met "wetland" criteria. Lucas then found himself stuck with a farm he could not work. Fields growing alfalfa tight to the wetland boundary were producing five to six tons per acre. Lucas argued that alfalfa will die out in soils that contain excessive amounts of moisture. Two adjoining fields in their sixth year of production had consistently yielded up to six tons of alfalfa annually.

On Steve Lucas's behalf, some other people wrote letters to Rick Donaldson with the U.S. Army Corps of Engineers.

Ernest Miller said he'd been involved with his family's operation of the land now owned by Lucas from 1922 till 1945. He said during those years " . . . we farmed and hayed the land which you now call wetlands." He explained ditches were built with horses and fresno scrapers to carry water for irrigation, and manure dams were built to help distribute the water.

Wesley Faupel wrote that he'd been hired by the Miller family in 1950, and that he'd worked there till 1981. He stated that Steve Lucas's land "has been farmed and typical haying practices have been used . . . almost every year . . . " He added the only way crops received water was by diverting irrigation ditches.

Henry Taylor bought the property in 1977. He wrote to the SCS in Winnemucca " . . . previous practices of operating the ranch by dragging all the fields in early spring" were continued. He referred to the "wetland" area as having had a "very inadequate water" supply.

Finally, in March of 1991, Range Conservationist Craig Plummer of the Winnemucca SCS office prepared an argument in favor of Steve Lucas and sent it to the Army Corps of Engineers in Sacramento. He began by introducing Lucas's original plan for the land: " . . . we are requesting that the U.S. Army Corps of Engineers, Regulatory Section, determine if land leveling or land smoothing in a farmed wetland is exempt under Section 404(f) of the Clean Water Act (normal farming activities exemption). Steve Lucas, owner of the 101 Ranch near Paradise Valley, Nevada, would like to level or smooth about 67 acres of farmed wetland (48 acres have been leveled before and 19 acres have never been leveled, but both have produced an agricultural commodity)."

Why was this request for a determination even needed? The SCS should certainly have been able to read and interpret a very clear definition in the Clean Water Act of "normal farming operations." If not, the Corps had already published a "Special Public Notice" in May of 1990 that listed plowing as normal, then defined plowing as " . . . all mechanical means of manipulating soil, including land leveling, to prepare it for the planting of crops."

Additionally, references by Mr. Plummer to "farmed wetland" were inappropriate because the Corps had released their own "Regulatory Guidance Letter" in September of 1990, stating farmed wetlands include areas with "15 or more consecutive days . . . of inundation during the growing season." The *Federal Manual for Identifying and Delineating Jurisdictional Wetlands* says inundation is when " . . . water temporarily or permanently covers a land surface." Plummer did argue that Steve Lucas's property was never inundated during a normal precipitation year.

But then everybody already knew that. So why was this even happening? Steve Lucas only wanted to level a dry field—to *save about five acre inches of irrigation water!* In his own letter to Rick Donaldson at the Corps of Engineers, Lucas explained that his leveling operation was never intended to move more than two inches of soil—that it could more appropriately be labeled "land smoothing."

Lucas included in his letter two more interesting notes: one, that a loan was outstanding against the property, and that the annual payment depended on full production of his land; and secondly (but perhaps more importantly), that Lucas had testified three months earlier before the State Sub-Committee to Study the "Takings" Order, and would be reporting back to them any decision of the Corps.

Lucas sent his letter on February 28, 1991.

On March 25, 1991, Walter Lamb, District Conservationist, sent some "new" findings to the Corps in Sacramento. He said he had "taken another look" at information regarding the 101 Ranch. He said he had determined that the 67 acres should be changed from "farmed wetland" to "prior converted wetland," based on three criteria: one, the land was leveled prior to December 23, 1985; two, an agricultural commodity had been produced in the area since 1982; and finally, the area had never been abandoned.

One day later, Robert Junell, Unit Chief of the Regulatory Section of the U.S. Army Corps of Engineers in Sacramento, issued a formal ruling: " . . . we concur that the 67 acres Mr. Lucas proposes to level are prior converted farmlands. Therefore, a Department of Army Permit will not be required."

In the two-year process of this battle that never should have happened, Steve Lucas spent $5,000 in legal fees. He saw his land depreciate by $250 an acre. Gross production loss on the 67 acres is calculated in excess of $60,000.

Lucas would like to know why wetlands interpretations are different between the different agencies? And most importantly, who pays for Soil Conservation Service errors?

(Steve Lucas does—and hundreds more like him.)

The outcome of the improper determination on the 101 Ranch was much more favorable than many others across the country; at least Steve Lucas was able to begin working his land. Many never do.

The key phrase here is "his land."

It's *not* really *his land* anytime a federal agency sets an eye to it. The government has at its disposal numerous tools to see to this, including (but not limited to) legislation, designations, condemnations, confiscations, foreclosures, evictions, "takings", illegal harassment and intimidation, "legal" blackmail, and complicity between agencies.

(If one don't getcha, the other one will).

Many federal bureaucrats do not care about such moral and basic things as private property rights. As far as they are concerned, "property rights" do not exist, and they will do all they can to remind landowners of that as often as possible. It is especially bothersome to most agency powercrats when they are faced with something they cannot control—hence, the need to "identify" such resources as wetlands and then *control* them.

Most farmers and ranchers are very caring stewards of the land, and they know and appreciate the value of wildlife within their own ecosystems. There are exceptions, of course, when jillions of blackbirds bombard a cornfield or when herds of elk trample a hay crop. But farmers know that water is a priceless commodity, and the management of their own pastures and fields is best left to those who depend on the land for survival. They have no desire to destroy it. Blatant offenders are easily spotted.

In defense of *all* property owners on the verge of becoming little more than tenants, a couple of courageous state lawmakers in Arizona cosponsored ground-breaking legislation in 1992. Senator Gus Arzberger and Representative Mark Killian co-wrote a bill that would protect property owners from losing their lands through hasty government action, and guaranteed fair compensation for loss of property or the use thereof.

The House and Senate each passed the bill. Governor Fife Symington was told by staffers and state agency heads they would resign if he signed this basic property rights legislation into law. Public outcry was heard statewide. Forty-six different organizations teamed up in support of the measure. Unlikely alliances emerged (Teamsters Union and Farm Bureau), lobbying Symington to sign the bill.

He did.

No sooner was the act complete when a coalition of left wing environmental interests began collecting petition signatures to force a referendum on the new law. They spread out rapidly across the state, calling their group "Take Back Your Rights"—duping voters out of their signatures by projecting a positive image of their negative intent.

They successfully collected enough valid voter signatures to force a referendum on the measure in 1994. With more than two dozen other states following Arizona's lead in property rights protection, environmentalist organizations across the nation placed Arizona at the bulls-eye of their target. Committed to spending millions of dollars on an intense propaganda campaign, they began referring to the Private Property Protection Act of 1992 as "the polluters' bill." A victory for them would set an important precedent and make an example of Arizona. Other states, then, might be less determined to follow suit.

While the law was awaiting the 1994 public vote, numerous groups accelerated efforts to claim large blocks of private lands. The Arizona Rivers Coalition went straight to the U.S. Congress (hoping to circumvent lengthy public comment periods), lobbying for swift passage of "Wild and Scenic" designations on 40 Arizona streams. The Arizona State Land Department (pressured by riparian interests) began a "study of navigability and property ownership" on the Gila, Salt, Verde, San Pedro and Hassayampa Rivers. Both of these actions were carefully orchestrated to take control of thousands of acres of private land operated by farmers, ranchers and others deriving their livelihoods from the bounty of the earth.

Just as with Steve Lucas and his fight for "possession" of the 101 Ranch in Nevada, the only defense for landowners is a concerted and *collective* front against the aggressors. To be passive is to lose the battle (along with many basic rights and freedoms). Nothing is granted. The extremists and bureaucrats will not relax in their push to take it all.

IV. **The Spoelstra Affair in Snohomish County**

John Spoelstra's dairy farm was repossessed by Farmers Home Administration—not for lack of productivity, but resulting from the faulty installation of a new pipeline and milking equipment.

The 1985 Farm Bill included a provision allowing a previous owner first right to buy back a repossessed property. When John Spoelstra attempted to so, he found that a couple of government agencies had been fast at work to justify claiming the property.

Matt Brady, District Conservationist at the Field Office of the Soil Conservation Service in Everett, Washington, had sent notice to FmHA that of the total 135 acres on Spoelstra's farm, "125 are classified as wetlands." That was March 31, 1988.

In less than two months, Acting Field Supervisor for the Fish and Wildlife Service in Olympia, Lynn P. Childers, had prepared an in-depth and detailed (eight-page, single-spaced) document supporting Brady's determination. Packed with legal interpretations, scientific findings, directives and recommendations, this document, too, was mailed to FmHA on May 27, 1988.

By way of definition, Childers wrote that the proposed easement (all 125 acres) was " . . . all those lands lying within the 100 year floodplain . . . (and that) floodplain and wetlands are synonymous . . . " Childers then examined (in the document) "Riparian Zones," "Endangered Species" and "Fish and Wildlife Habitats." The following are chronologically listed reasons why John Spoelstra should be deprived of the use of all but ten acres of his farm:

(1) "Two areas of riparian vegetation persist along property boundaries. The first area borders Ebey Slough . . . (and) is of particular importance because it provides shade . . . for migrating salmon . . . "

(2) "The second area forms about one-half of the west property boundary. Vegetation along this slough provides protective cover for waterfowl and . . . quail."

(3) "The entire Snohomish/Ebey/Steamboat delta is known to support good numbers of wintering bald eagles. A bald eagle has perched on the neighboring property . . . "

(4) " . . . the site is frequented by sensitive species such as northern harriers and red-tailed hawks."

(Remember, this is not a study of *public* land; this is still private property.)

Covenants by the landowner (written in Childers' document) included a ban on the building of any dwellings, barns or outbuildings on the land, and a contradictory directive not to alter the vegetation in any way and, at the same time, maintain " . . . control of noxious or other undesirable plants on the easement area." Further, the landowner was not to allow cattle or other stock on the easement.

Displaying an attitude common to Fish and Wildlife agents, Lynn Childers then wrote: "The United States, on behalf of itself, at its sole discretion, (reserves) the right of ingress and egress to conduct easement management . . . and enforcement activities. The easement manager may utilize any . . . route of access . . . (but) the landowner may provide a designated route to and from the easement area so that damage . . . can be . . . avoided."

The government also reserved the right to install and maintain structures (Spoelstra could not) and to manipulate vegetation (Spoelstra could not), to construct fences to prevent "encroachment" and to exclude landowner entry (while Spoelstra *owns* the land and pays the taxes on it).

On behalf of John Spoelstra, Ed Soper of the Washington Farm and Land Company wrote a letter to Congressman Al Swift in March of 1989, explaining that Spoelstra's farm contains the most productive soils in all of Snohomish County. He listed the distribution of the various types of alluvial soils prime for the production of peas, corn, berries, forage, specialty crops and vegetables.

He pointed out the farm had been in agricultural production for 100 years. The only valid justification for claiming the acreage as wetland was the presence of canary grass and bulrush. Soper projected lost economics based on a potential population of 110 cows for 110 acres, exceeding $615,000 and 22 jobs, including necessary support services to a dairyman. He added that the Spoelstra farm contributed more than $4,000 to the Snohomish County Diking District annually, and argued finally that the "safety net" built into the 1985 Farm Bill (allowing a farmer to buy his farm back) was intended to preserve the family farm, not destroy it by taking away the land that makes it work.

Copies of Ed Soper's letter were mailed to Congressman Tom Foley, Senator Slade Gorton, the Washington State Director of FmHA, and others.

Four months later, in July of 1989, SCS District Conservationist Matt Brady (the same guy who got this all started) wrote to Ray Kulina, Snohomish County Supervisor for FmHA: "A quality assurance review of my March 31, 1988, HEL/Wetland Determination on this property found it to be incorrect . . . " He cited new findings in inundation and abandonment criteria, none of which had ever been at issue.

In sharing this episode with officials at the American Farm Bureau Federation in 1991, Darrell Turner, President of the Washington State Farm Bureau, reported an interesting side story. He said a portion of the Snohomish River Valley had been designated "agricultural" some years before when the Snohomish County Council developed a "comprehensive plan for the county." Property owners then paid tax assessments for dike and drainage ditch maintenance, which the county did.

John Spoelstra's farm lay in the middle of the district. Fish and Wildlife officials refused to pay the assessments for ditch maintenance or to clean their portion of the ditch themselves. Other farmers found their properties "involuntarily converted to wetlands" because their fields could no longer drain properly. At a hearing concerning these events, FmHA regional officials refused to hear testimony from State Senator Cliff Bailey, who was Chairman of the County Council when the district was designated agricultural.

Darrell Turner writes emphatically, "This is not the sort of 'democracy' I care to support."

His words echo the sentiments of thousands.

Marion Kryger of Vermillion, South Dakota, expresses anger at being duped into signing the wetlands declaration, and adds, "Who did the determination and by what reasoning? They say one thing and do another—my photos reflect how dumb they are!!"

George Eidsness of Brocker, North Dakota, says, "The ASC delayed making a decision on my drainage. I was led to believe it was approved . . . (then) the SCS notified me I was farming converted wetlands. I destroyed the 21 acres to avoid losing all government payments, plus some additional acreage to be sure I wasn't on converted wetlands . . . The ASC and SCS came out twice to stake the boundary of the converted wetlands . . . being unable to distinguish a difference . . . they will now take another aerial photo . . . "

Donnie Buckmier of Minnewaukan, North Dakota, writes, "The ditch . . . has been maintained through the ASCS office, but now has been dammed because of change of landowners, creating a wetland on my land. The ASCS finds this to their advantage."

Bob Cuister of Marlette, Michigan, went to sign up for a farm program and found that his acreage (which he'd farmed for many years) had been classified as wetland by the Fish and Wildlife Service, " . . . based solely on hydric soil."

Donald Jones of Belgrade, Montana, is rightfully confused: " . . . ASCS informed me I could not seed hay barley—SCS said I could. I question if it is really wetlands as water only runs through the place when farmers above me are irrigating . . . "

(Confusion seems to be a key ingredient in most of the stories.)

Don Rice of Clatskanie, Oregon, says, "Farmers are afraid to do maintenance work on their property for fear that they will be in violation of somebody's rule and be fined or go to jail. The rules are so numerous and complex that one can't begin to know them all, much less keep up on the changes and the various interpretations."

Carl Fritz of Guys Mills, Pennsylvania, adds, " . . . because of conflicting state and federal regulations, it makes it very difficult to know what is indeed allowable and which of the roughly seven agencies have jurisdiction over my property."

(Amazingly, farmers keep clinging to the antiquated belief that it is *their* property.)

Jim Hadwiger of Cherokee, Oklahoma, has long been a member and chairman of the American Farm Bureau Federation Wheat Advisory Committee. He observes, "The problem of improper determination is nationwide and has been a concern of almost every committee member . . . Some feel it is a move by Congress to save money by harassing farmers until they drop out of the farm program. It may be working."

The most germane voice of all is perhaps that of a 33-year veteran employee of the Soil Conservation Service. Merle Huhner of Devils Lake, North Dakota, sent a list of 45 Ramsey County farm operators with wetland determination problems to Herb Manig of the American Farm Bureau. He said any one of the individuals could give complete documentation of respective problems, and he concluded, " . . . I personally feel that present wetland regulations have arbitrarily encroached upon private property rights and have overreached in defining wetlands. The USDA, EPA, Corps of Engineers, FWS, and other government agencies have lost all perspective in efforts to regulate wetlands."

V. The Loudest Voices

It is difficult to believe this is happening in the United States of America. We are taught as children that our nation was founded on the basic principles of freedom and the pursuit of happiness. Is the American Dream still intact? A sad truth is, our Federal Government—by way of the enormous bureaucracies it has fostered—no longer subscribes to the philosophies of our founding fathers.

There are hundreds of lawmakers in Washington influenced by thousands of lobbyists from dozens of special interest groups who work very hard to get hundreds of new laws passed each year that serve only to restrict the freedoms of millions. More often than not, new laws are disguised as "amendments" to omnibus legislation, and the American public doesn't know the added restrictions are being considered until they're passed. Few politicians at the federal level vote the genuine will of their constituents back home. There are many reasons.

First and foremost, they are so removed from grassroots America that they don't know what the will of the people might be. Secondly, they somehow very quickly develop an attitude that being elected to Capitol Hill has blessed them with superior wisdom, and they know best of all what is good for their constituency. They become jaded, relishing the high life, black-tie dinners, expensive parties, limousines, airplanes and trips; it's easy to lose touch.

And they hear the loudest voices.

Those thousands of lobbyists _lobby_ for a living. They get up each morning—_every_ morning—and go to Capitol Hill. They do it with the same regularity and dedication that Steve Lucas tends his alfalfa and John Spoelstra milks his cows. It is their _job_.

Again, I repeat, there are tens of _thousands_ of them.

Lobbying entails many things—from conversations to lunches to dinners and parties to concessions to trade-offs to personal promises to very influential and cleverly managed campaign contributions. Lobbyists know better than anyone the value in Calvin Coolidge's famous quote: "Nothing in this world can take the place of persistence." If you pry at a closed door long enough with enough different tools, eventually something will break it open.

Lobbyists work for private companies, industry, unions, business, other governments, environmentalist groups, and agencies within the U.S. Government itself. It's not uncommon for lobbyists to come from several directions on a particular issue and work as a team. When a cluster of farmers in rural America organize a letter-writing campaign through their local Farm Bureau in an effort to counter the pressure applied by the Environmental Protection Agency, the U.S. Fish and Wildlife Service, the Audubon Society and the Sierra Club, who do you think is heard?

Whose voice is loudest?

The Sierra Club alone has nearly 600,000 members, and they maintain their own legal defense fund. Most of those members did not join the environmentalist movement to stop farmers from working their fields, but their numbers (and annual dues) support the ones who lobby in Washington and pursue pernicious lawsuits.

Everyone has an agenda.

In our "free" United States, there are more than 500 separate environmental protectionist associations. They range from the Roo Rat Society to the Beaver Defenders, from the Birds of Prey Rehabilitation Foundation to the Defenders of Wildlife. They are all dedicated to defending *something*. This is all fine in spirit, but inevitably the zealots allow no compromise for the "rights" of others—especially landowners.

Then, there are the environmental foundations and funding sources. These operate under such trustworthy names as Friends of the Earth Foundation and The Nature Conservancy. There are 145 of them in the United States.

There are more than 350 federal government organizations, 59 of them within the Department of the Interior. The DOI, of course, is the mother of the Bureau of

Land Management, the Fish and Wildlife Service, the Land and Renewable Resources Department, the National Park Service, and among many others, the Office of Environmental Affairs. To the private landowner with no agenda but the well-being of his family and a livelihood generated through the wise management of a small acreage, this bureaucracy begins soon to resemble a house of horrors.

Add to these another 117 independent agencies and commissions. It's more than a little frightening to find out the Environmental Protection Agency (EPA) falls within this group. This so-called watchdog agency has _50 different divisions_, each one with its own director and staff! Compare the names of these two different divisions: the Office of Toxic Substances, Environmental Assistance Division, and the Office of Toxic Substances, Health and Environmental Review Division (each with a director and staff). There are six divisions dealing with _water_ (each with a director and staff).

Somebody approved this. Somebody allowed it to happen. Somebody is funding this monolith of the bureaucracy business.

Remember, the EPA is an _independent agency_ with no one controlling it but its own directors. In 1993, EPA Director Carolyn Browner said she intended to make her agency more "feared" by the American public than the IRS. There is no electoral accountability here. And Congress is moving to give the EPA cabinet status in 1994—equal to the Department of Defense!

Have you guessed yet what we've been missing through all of this? Lest we forget: _state_ agencies and commissions and organizations and foundations and associations and governments.

And thousands more lobbyists and special interests.

Just as tilling the soil is a means of livelihood and a culture unto itself, so is the work of lobbyists and bureaucrats. There are those within numerous agencies who go off to work each morning _knowing_ they are going to ruin someone's life. They do not care; it is their job—their way of life. Just as the farmer with a bumper crop, they are proud when they do their jobs well.

This country was founded by men and women (the ones we mentioned who believed in freedom) who knew the burden of too much government—of over-taxation, invasions of property and rights, unfair "takings" and restrictions. Somewhere along the way since those honorable beginnings, somebody has forgotten.

A sad commentary within our society is that we've conditioned ourselves to take what the elected (and self-appointed) rulemakers dish out. Rebellion is no longer an acceptable recourse—but it should be. Early in 1993, U.S. Senator John McCain told a group of concerned citizens in Safford, Arizona, that if environmental issues continued to compound the lives of rural Americans, there would be "a revolution in the West."

An amazing thing that has evolved within our society is the degree of patience, tolerance, endurance and civility displayed by the multitudes of landowners who are kicked around by bureaucrats. A hundred years ago it would have happened only once, but we are again conditioned—*reconciled*—to allowing ourselves to be abused by those we perceive to have more authority.

These are real people with dreams and goals and ambitions who believed in "the American Way." They have withstood debt and taxes and hardship in order to own a piece of ground and make independent choices about personal management. Our Constitution encourages and supports these kinds of activities. Nowhere in the documents establishing a framework for this nation is there a single provision allowing for anything like the activities of the EPA, the SCS, and other agencies too numerous to name.

If current trends are allowed to continue, the backbone of the greatest country in the world can (and *will)* be broken—not by an external blow, but by a deadly cancer eating at it from within. (Subsequent chapters of this book show how widespread the epidemic already is.)

Honest Americans are the victims here, and only honest Americans can stop this push for complete government control.

VI. **The Nightmare Continues in Waves**

Wayne Domingue of Lafayette, Louisiana, obtained 100% financing from a local banker to clean up 35 acres of his land and convert it from a public trash dump to a freshwater impoundment for raising crawfish. He developed the area and began harvesting crawfish. Eighteen months later, Domingue was contacted by the Army Corps of Engineers and told he was in violation of the Clean Water Act. For two-and-a-half years, he battled "every working minute" with agencies from the Corps to the SCS to the EPA to the U.S. Fish and Wildlife Service to save his enterprise. In the process, he lost everything, including his home. His property is now "worthless."

Dan Witmer of Orrville, Ohio, cleared some briars from a good productive field in order to maximize crop potential. He is now ineligible for USDA benefits if he farms the field. Use of the land would decrease the value of his farm.

Robert Coppinger of Manson, Iowa, wished to change a channel to mitigate damages caused by an unpermitted levee and channel change downstream. The government refused to allow Coppinger to do the work. He went through a three-day DNR appeal hearing and an appeal before the Iowa Environmental Protection Commission. The EPA finally overruled staff and granted a 401 certification. The Corps held onto the certification for several months, delaying a 404 permit due to opposition from the Fish and Wildlife Service. Even if all this was suddenly resolved, a minimal effect determination pending for over two years still had not been granted by the SCS. The SCS demanded 16 acres of wetland mitigation for one net acre of stream channel loss. Legal costs have exceeded $20,000, and the value of the 160-acre farm has decreased by more than $500 per acre—a total loss of over $100,000.

Domenick DelVecchio of North Kingstown, Rhode Island, filled in a wet pasture area in 1968. Rhode Island passed a wetland law in 1972. The Corps of Engineers 404 permitting process came the following year. In 1984, DelVecchio refilled the sunken spots in his then productive pasture. He was cited with a cease and desist order from the Soil Conservation Service and the State Department of Environmental Management, and ordered to remove all fill and restore the land to pre-1960 condition. After six years, the issue was still unresolved and DelVecchio could no longer afford the legal fees.

Annie James of Humboldt, Tennessee, found her 700-acre woodland inundated by water backed up behind beaver dams. She was not allowed to drain her property, and the timber died.

Larry Fore of Latta, South Carolina, tore down an old tobacco-curing barn in 1990. He had owned his farm for 25 years and, as regulations required, he reported his action to the ASCS office. He then found out that the precise spot where the barn had stood (an area 20 feet by 30 feet) was classified as wetland with no basis for the determination provided. Fore says the area has never stood water, and no one would build a tobacco-curing barn on a spot that was not well-drained. The crumbling structure had stood at the edge of a field, and now Fore must plant around the 20x30 spot. And for moving the barn, he faces thousands of dollars in lost subsidies and loans.

Joe McMichael of Spencerville, Ohio, bought an 80-acre field in 1976. He wanted to clear 16 acres of "woods" from the field in 1989 to crop the entire area in soybeans, corn and wheat. The Soil Conservation Service ruled the woods a wetland. The decision was appealed all the way to Washington, and summarily denied. McMichael had purchased equipment to clear the woodlands. The equipment was idled and the ground untouchable. After two years of fighting, McMichael had lost $9,000 in income, $36,800 in land devaluation, and $15,000 in equipment costs.

S. Thomas Hart of Chesapeake, Virginia, bought seven parcels of woodland ranging from four acres to 36 acres each. It was well-drained land. Hart sold the timber in preparation for clearing the land to use as a farm. The Swampbuster Act was passed part way through this process, and Hart was not allowed to clear his property. He decided to build a retirement home on a 20-acre parcel, and gave three additional parcels to his children for building homes of their own. The Army Corps of Engineers received an anonymous complaint that Tommy Hart was clearing wetlands. A couple of engineers came to investigate and found the allegation to be untrue. Hart revealed that he wanted to build a home on the property. The engineers said he could not because the parcel was within a half-mile of the Northwest River. Hart protested. The engineers later decided that Hart _could_ build if his land was 7.2 feet above sea level because his land was now being considered a subdivision and he the developer. Hart explained that his land had been surveyed into parcels 100 years ago. The engineers stated simply that they considered the property all one parcel because all the parcels were adjoining. Hart then received a letter from the COE that he would not be allowed to sell off any portion of his land or he would lose the approval he'd been given for a single permit to build a single house. Hart asked a COE supervisor why he was being singled out. The supervisor said no one else had been complained on (even though the complaint was erroneous). Hart's six parcels have been made useless to him, he has spent $20,000 in legal costs, and the value of the property has decreased by $150,000.

William Stamp, Jr., of Cranston, Rhode Island, planned to sell farmland for industrial use as determined by the city in 1965. Excessive and illogical regulations from the State Department of Environmental Management and the Corps of Engineers prevented the sale and development of the property (although it was zoned "industrial"). The DEM demanded nine acres of Stamp's prime property in exchange for allowing the project to proceed. Even lawyers could not understand the demands of the COE. Over-taxation and land devaluation nixed any chance of making a sale. The same burdens forced Stamp to forfeit his land. Property value decreased from $3.80 per square foot to absolutely nothing. Debt, debt services and professional fees amounted to $3,000,000. Stamp said the impact on family health and the amount of pain and suffering incurred since the industrial zoning in 1965 were "incomprehensible." Stamp was told by his attorney that an assistant U.S. attorney had intimated that by contacting senators and congressmen in this matter, Stamp had made matters worse for himself. Stamp says the regulatory agencies have been given a license to steal private property. He concludes, "The only means not used *so far* in order to achieve their goal is the use of artillery!"

VII. The Art of Legal Hostage-Taking

A common denominator exists within all the stories detailed thus far in this book. All the landowners were deprived of the right to make sensible, wise management decisions on land they considered their own. The federal government had imposed these restrictions upon them by passing into law certain provisions of the Food Security Act of 1985. That, in turn, set the Soil Conservation Service actively into motion "identifying" and classifying "wetlands" with no regard at all for the rights and livelihoods of property owners, or the heritage and traditions of entire cultures.

It's not likely that members of Congress envisioned (or intended) their "swampbuster" legislation to result in designated wetlands occupying tiny patches in the center of farmed fields. The SCS has interpreted and acted upon the mandate so capriciously that thousands of wetlands now exist in previously productive agricultural areas that have never been "wet." These findings were based on data as inconclusive as aerial photos with unexplained shadows, the presence of a maverick weed, and sometimes no evidence at all. Thousands of appeals by desperate farmers and ranchers have been summarily denied by low-ranking bureaucrats, agency heads and the courts. The determinations were made, and the landowners simply lost their rights.

The legislation included a built-in provision for the bureaucracy to make legal "hostages" of any property owners who might choose to defy this newly found control—*take away farm program benefits.* The traditional five-year Farm Bill has provided various benefits over the years with programs designed to mold and shape the agriculture industry. Farmers have been paid to take land out of production, or specific crops have been subsidized to help maintain balance. These programs become mandates that put some farmers "over a barrel," so to speak, especially when they are threatened with losing benefits they've been encouraged to depend on.

When the farmer loses his land *and* his benefits, he's out of business. Therefore, he is forced to comply with decisions, determinations, designations and denials made by bureaucrats who don't care about his survival. He is not permitted any longer to think of his land as *his land.* While he still withstands the burdens of debt and taxes and maintenance, he must think of the land as belonging to the controlling agency. He must live by their management decisions, even if it means hardship and ultimate failure.

VIII. On the Return Road to Feudalism

The American Dream was conceived through a particular concept of "property rights." Everything about the founding and settling of this young nation—organized land grabs, claim-staking, homesteading, "nesting," opening and colonizing the West (all approved by a fledgling democratic government)—was based on a perception of inalienable property rights. The quest for the Western World was largely inspired by an abundance of oppressive restrictions and heavy-handed government control plied to citizens not allowed to *own* property in the "old countries" of Europe.

Dr. Bruce Yandle, Alumni Professor of Legal Studies at Clemson University, notes that it took 500 years for ordinary men and women of medieval Europe to escape a system called "feudalism"—where serfs worked the land controlled by the government and a lord of the manor. As a new civilization crept onto the eastern shores of North America, a form of government was created to protect the rights of the people. Safeguards were built into the system by way of constitutional guarantees that would guard the people and their rights from the government itself.

Property rights were at the very base of all this. The U.S. Constitution treats property rights as the most basic civil right of all. Professor Yandle says, "When civil rights to property are not protected, all other rights are endangered."

In June of 1989, the Sacramento law firm of Downey, Brand, Seymour and Rohwer wrote some clarifications of the "swampbuster" provisions of the Food Security Act of 1985. The Glenn-Colusa Irrigation District at Willows, California, had asked for a clearer understanding of the fine points of the law. In summary, attorney David Lindgren wrote, "The only activity prohibited by the swampbuster provisions . . . is the actual growing of *annual* crops on wetlands converted after 1985. They do not, for example, prohibit the destruction of wetlands. If crops are grown on converted wetlands, the penalty imposed . . . is the loss of most federal crop program benefits for all crops for the year in question."

If only it were that simple.

Ocie and Carey Mills of Navarre, Florida, know better. They each served nearly two years in a federal penitentiary—and were fined a total of $10,000—for placing 19 loads of clean construction sand on a lot less than a half-acre in size. The area was a "designated wetland" on their property, and they did not get a Corps of Engineers permit.

John Pzsgai of Morristown, Pennsylvania, removed some old tires, junked car bodies and other garbage from his land bordering a creek. He brought in top soil to replace the debris. He was found guilty of "disturbing a wetland," and spent nearly three years in prison. Released in late 1992, John was ordered to restore the creek bank to its original condition, including the tires and car parts.

Bill Ellen, a dedicated wildlife preservationist, was building a series of duck ponds on his Maryland property. He was convicted of "filling a wetland." He spent six months in jail, four months in home detention and a full year under supervised release.

These individuals are not criminals. They have all paid dearly, however, for making the fateful mistake of trying to _improve_ their properties. Their "most basic civil right" was ignored and stripped away. Now, their lives have been altered, they endure enormous financial responsibilities, and they are felons (which precipitates the loss of numerous other rights).

Professor Yandle points out there has always been tension between the holders of rights to land and the government organized to protect those rights. He adds that land (or the rights to it) can be taken away with greater ease than most other assets because it (they) can be taken silently. For example, when irrigation water is restricted for one reason or another, it affects the value of farms previously accustomed to having that water. If land cannot be used because of wetlands or endangered species designations, the landowner alone bears the financial brunt because these "takings" are done without compensation.

True takings—when a highway department acquires right-of-way across private property, for instance—are paid for, based on some estimation of fair value. While this is not necessarily a road free of potholes, it at least complies with rights guaranteed by the Fifth Amendment to the Constitution—that private property cannot be taken for public purpose without compensation.

New laws either passed or being considered in over half of the states (including the one under special-interest referendum in Arizona) require that legislators assess the impact of their actions on private property before passing further restrictive legislation. Environmental groups and regulatory agencies oppose this thinking vehemently; they don't want the potential results of their lobbying scrutinized that closely. The efforts of the intrepid state lawmakers who *are* listening to their constituents on this issue can only be applauded as a good beginning.

But why is it necessary that individual state governments must attempt to reassert basic rights that remain "guaranteed" in the U.S. Constitution? Professor Yandle says the erosion of personal rights began with the very government invented to protect them.

IX. **Death of Common Law and Birth of Regulation**

Yandle explains the beginning of the burgeoning snowball that now threatens all the basic civil rights upon which "free" Americans have learned to base their lives: ". . . common law, transported from England, formed the foundation of our legal system. It was the law of the land."

Then, the holder of a deed to a parcel of land could feel secure in his rights. Yandle says that under the common law system, there was respect for the landowner: "If someone upstream discharged waste that polluted the water passing by a downstream property holder . . . the common law remedy was simple. The upstream discharger had to stop."

There was no question or argument about it. Rights were protected.

Yandle points out that common law courts were far from perfect, but they practiced an attitude that was healthy for individuals with rights. First of all, in order to bring a lawsuit before the court, a plaintiff had to show some evidence of damages. More important, individual courts and judges could not issue orders that affected every landowner in the country; they dealt only with the parties to the controversy. Under that system, special interest groups could not possibly lobby all the judges to obtain widespread similar rulings on cases brought before the courts.

However, Congress *can* pass laws that affect everyone in the country. Also, legislative bodies can impose statutes based on "damages" that have no sound basis.

Armed with this knowledge, special interest groups and the losing parties in some common law court battles sought to gain their ends through the legislature. Until the late 1800s, the Congress was restricted by the Supreme Court in matters relating to market regulation. Then Congress passed the Act to Regulate Commerce, and established the Interstate Commerce Commission. It was 1887—the year of the eternal gift of victory for special interests and power-hungry bureaucrats who operate under the guise of "serving the public interest" to achieve their own objectives.

Professor Yandle says, "With broad interpretation made of the Commerce Clause, legislation gave birth to regulation, and regulation yielded a permanent bureaucracy supported by special interest groups who no longer had to pay for changes they desired. Statutes eroded the power of the common law courts. Concern over what is termed the public interest—which generally means *special* interest—replaced concern for private interests. Regulation expanded and with it came a deterioration of property rights to land."

The late Dixy Lee Ray, former Governor of Washington and former Chairwoman of the Atomic Energy Commission, said the preservation of private property is "imperative" because the government is slowly taking it away.

The government currently controls more than a third of the land area within the United States. That amount is growing every day. Another 17 percent of U.S. soil is held by other levels of government—states and municipalities.

By mid-1994, the total figure was approaching *50 percent!*

Ray believed the federal government guilty of using the Clean Water Act and the Endangered Species Act to broadly *take* private property. Ray stated that federal regulators use Section 404 of the Clean Water Act to "identify" wetlands and bring them under federal control.

Ironically, no federal law exists with respect to wetlands. All that's specifically stated in the Clean Water Act is that the Army Corp of Engineers has the right to regulate the discharge of "dredged spoils into navigable waters . . . "

That's *all* there is there!

Governor Ray said those words have been "twisted and twisted to subsume a definition of wetland that has been interpreted in about 50 different ways." Perhaps the broadest interpretation is the classifying as "wetland" any land where the water underground rises to within a foot-and-a-half of the surface for a period of five consecutive days during any given year.

What has this to do with "dredged spoils" or "navigable waters?"

Lawmakers have never been able to agree on what constitutes a wetland. The 1987 wetlands delineation manual defined wetlands as land that is wet on the surface for at least 12.5 percent of the growing season. However, a 1989 manual superseded the earlier version, and stated that lands only had to be inundated for a week out of the year to be considered wetlands. A furor arose as a result of the latter definition, so a third version was written in 1991. The period of inundation was lengthened to 15 days, or saturation of the surface for 21 days. Understandably now, environmental extremists and regulation-mad bureaucrats alike objected because this seemed like a loss of ground to them. The Bush Administration chose not to tangle with these interests and left it all as a gift to the incoming Clinton camp, which reverted to the original manual of 1987 for the duration of a National Academy of Sciences "study" costing about $400,000.

There's still no federal law allowing for the kinds of wetlands "takings" exercised by the Environmental Protection Agency, the Army Corps of Engineers, the Fish and Wildlife Service, the Soil Conservation Service and others who cannot agree on what a wetland really is.

The determinations are made (and property owners' lives ruined) by greedy little bureaucrats who carry the clout of uncontrolled federal agencies with them. Their actions are summarily sanctioned by more powerful bureaucrats and some courts. The basic civil right of property rights belonging to the property owner is not a consideration in these matters.

To the bureaucrats, regulators, preservation extremists and unfettered federal agencies who believe all is not well unless all is under their control, nothing really counts except the broadening of their control. Dixy Lee Ray said when they win one battle, they just go on to another, bit by bit, taking control and eroding personal rights and freedoms. Commonly, the rare plants, endangered animals, critical habitats, et cetera, used to stop development or improved management on private land are only "excuses"—a means to an end.

Howard Hutchinson, legal researcher and technical advisor for the Coalition of Arizona/New Mexico Counties, says, "The government is not the answer for protecting the environment—indeed, the U.S. government is the worst spoiler of the environment that has ever been." He adds that the ever-continuing acquisition of private land by the federal government (and the accompanying extermination of personal rights and freedoms) is a "slow strangulation as opposed to clubbing someone over the head."

II.

THE MOST ENDANGERED SPECIES— MANKIND

I. **Where Eagles Die**

In late March of 1993, federal officials conducted a raid on the Montana ranch of Paul and Rosie Berger. Officers from the U.S. Fish and Wildlife Service and the Bureau of Land Management (16 of them altogether) took no chances with this one. They went in armed and wearing flak jackets. In support of their assault, they employed a half-dozen 4-wheel-drive vehicles, an airplane with two agents aboard, three people on a "chemical team," additional ground crew, an attorney, other agents from the Montana Fish and Wildlife Department and the BLM, and a camera crew from Cable Network News (CNN).

Local officials were not informed that a raid was planned. No local news coverage was allowed at the scene. Garland County Sheriff Charles Phipps and one deputy arrived at the ranch only after being called by one of Berger's neighbors.

Paul Berger, 71, and his 81-year-old wife Rosie were accused of poisoning eagles. They were not advised of their rights, nor were they allowed to call an attorney during the search of their property. Some farm chemicals were confiscated, as were two pickup trucks. The remains of some dead birds were collected and sent to a government lab in Oregon.

What had the appearance of a major crime bust at first now became little more than a circumstantial case. The lab in Oregon identified two bird carcasses as varieties of hawk and gull. Forensic experts could not find evidence of poisoning in the birds (including the remains of two eagles). A second raid by 50 agents on BLM-managed land leased by Berger—complete with aerial flyovers in grid patterns—turned up nothing.

Berger remained charged with illegally taking up to 17 eagles under the Eagle Act, the Migratory Bird Treaty Act and the Endangered Species Act. He was also charged with the use of carbofuran "inconsistent with its labeling" under the Federal Insecticides Act. Conviction on these charges could result in prison time and hundreds of thousands of dollars in fines. Berger's defense disputed his client being charged with the same crime three times by three different governmental agencies, but U.S. Magistrate Richard Anderson of Billings let the charges stand.

Three former employees of the Berger Ranch testified against Paul Berger. Tanya Jones said she had watched her employer take a container of liquid from a shop and later pour some on a lamb carcass. Two cousins, Paul Booth and Vernon Austin, painted verbal pictures for the jury of incidents that would suggest Berger's intent to poison eagles that were killing his lambs.

Jones said she had left Berger's employ because he had patted her "on the bottom" and she was too embarrassed to face him with it. Booth and Austin left amid a dispute over wages, a stolen microwave oven and some tools.

A government trapper, the county trapper and the BLM range conservationist all testified they had never seen any dead eagles on the Berger Ranch.

In late August, 1993, the jury acquitted Paul Berger of the charges involving the alleged death of eagles by poisoning. He was convicted of using a pesticide in a manner inconsistent with its labeling.

No one has ever said Paul Berger should not have been punished if, in fact, he was maintaining a consistent practice of poisoning eagles. But how can the show of force by officials serving the initial warrant for search and seizure on the Berger property be justified?

Paul and Rosie Berger were elderly, alone, and in failing health. They put up no resistance. Paul Berger voluntarily took the agents to his shed containing pesticides.

Why 20 men, armed and wearing bulletproof vests?

Sheriff Phipps said, "When they invite the national media and not inform the local law enforcement, then I think it's a power show in front of the cameras."

The raid was planned and executed on the strength of an 800-number phone tip from Vernon Austin—a convicted felon who had just lost his job at the Berger Ranch.

Many residents around Sand Springs speculate that federal agents *wanted* a gun battle. Edwin Clark of Brusett thinks one might have happened had Sheriff Phipps and his deputy not shown up quickly. Assistant U.S. Attorney Kris McLean (accompanying the first armed raiders) wore a cap that day emblazoned with the initials "ATF." The same caps were worn by Alcohol, Tobacco and Firearms agents during a deadly raid at about the same time on the Branch Davidian sect in Waco, Texas.

Sheriff Phipps said, "They could have notified me, and I could have gone in there and served the warrant. There wouldn't have been any guns pulled."

The second raid upon Berger's holdings was concentrated solely on the BLM lease-permit lands adjacent to Berger's own property. Defense Attorney Jay Lansing maintained in court that this operation—considering the high intensity of manpower and the enormous cost—was strictly punitive in nature, the single objective being to cancel Berger's BLM permits if anything was found.

It all might have worked had the entire operation not been so sloppy. But then again, Paul Berger's salvation might well have been having his case heard before a jury of Montanans—folks who are becoming less impressed with the highhanded tactics of presumptuous government officials and more concerned about the preservation of basic civil rights.

A common approach used by federal agencies in their ever-widening quest for power and control is to instill fear into those who might oppose them. The Internal Revenue Service has done it, and the Environmental Protection Agency. In this case, the U.S. Fish and Wildlife Service attempted to make "examples" of an aging couple in Montana. It didn't work.

Unfortunately, there have been other cases that did . . . and there will be more.

II. **Roo Rats Rule in Riverside County**

Michael Rowe of Winchester, California, had worked long and hard to scrape together the money he needed to build a home of adequate size to accommodate his family of five. While doing so, Rowe and his wife, along with their two teenaged sons and a younger daughter, were stuffed inside a one-bedroom house on their 20-acre "ranch" in rural Riverside County.

In 1991, Rowe decided to build. He applied for a permit and was promptly rejected. To his dismay, he was informed by a county official that his property lay within a "study area" for the endangered Stephens' kangaroo rat. He was told that any activity on his land that might injure or disturb the lemon-sized rodent could result in arrest, a federal prison sentence and up to $100,000 in fines.

Desperately needing enlarged living space for his family, Michael Rowe pursued the issue. Perhaps there were options available, avenues of approach that would allow him to circumvent this major roadblock.

There were.

Rowe was told he could hire a biologist to study his property. This would cost about $5,000. While the biological study was being conducted, Rowe would be left with no options at all—except perhaps prayer—because the discovery of a single rat would preclude any development on the property. If the land was found to be rat-free, then Michael Rowe could build a house for his family—providing he paid "mitigation fees" enabling the Fish and Wildlife Service to buy other land for the rat sanctuary. That would cost him about $40,000.

Rowe could not afford any part of the option. He was forced (under threat of going to prison) to leave his land undisturbed. His family continued to live in a one-bedroom house.

There are many such stories in Riverside County. Federal protection of the Stephens' kangaroo rat under the Endangered Species Act has idled about 78,000 acres of rural countryside, much of it privately owned. Property values have nose-dived, and many landowners who want to sell cannot.

Many of Michael Rowe's neighbors lost their homes to the devastating wildfires that swept through portions of southern California in late 1993. On behalf of the Stephens' rat, the Endangered Species Act had prevented landowners there from properly controlling the encroachment of coastal sage scrub around their homes. Uncut brush fueled the wildfires. Hundreds of acres burned, dozens of homes were lost.

Rowe's house did not burn.

He had applied for a permit to disc a firebreak around his home a year before the fires came. His request was denied by the FWS because he had not completed those expensive biological studies. As fire crawled over a nearby hill at 1:00 A.M., Rowe and his neighbor Ray Borell climbed aboard their tractors and turned a line of soil across their properties into a protective barrier. Their homes were saved, but in doing so, Rowe and Borell committed a crime for which they could be prosecuted.

This particular rodent (and the unwavering protection thereof) has affected Riverside County in other ways, too. An attempt by the Riverside National Cemetery (the only federal cemetery in southern California still accepting interments) to expand its boundaries resulted in the loss of 80 acres and $40,000 in fees. The cleanup of a contaminated rocket test site near Beaumont was delayed two years because rats might be disturbed.

Riverside County, California, is faced with protecting more endangered species than just kangaroo rats. An 18,000-acre preserve has been created near Palm Springs solely for the preservation of a fringe-toed lizard. Another retreat has been staked out for the least Bell's vireo. Meanwhile, property values continue to plummet and development is stymied.

Howard Hutchinson of the Coalition of Arizona/New Mexico Counties says, "The interesting thing about the Endangered Species Act is everybody views it with fear."

The behavior of the U.S. Fish and Wildlife Service in their interpretation and administration of the ESA has caused this to happen. Congress approved the ESA in 1973 with the intent of protecting some recognizable species known to be dwindling, but few envisioned it as a crusade for insects and weeds. Two decades ago, even as the law was being heralded as a "tough conservation law," no one would have believed that road-building in Montana would be delayed by grizzly bears, or that the timber industry throughout the West would be impaired by spotted owls.

This translates to lost jobs and damaged economies.

It was impossible to foresee then that an eyeless crustacean the size of a weevil could stop the construction of a prison and an airport in Virginia, or that a salamander and a gambusia could curtail 65 percent of the water supply to San Antonio, Texas.

Anyone—citizen or group—can petition the Fish and Wildlife Service to declare a species endangered. A review period follows. However, the "review" does not include any of the possible ways an "endangered" classification on a species might impact private property, economic development, existing customs and cultures, renewable resources, local industry or marketplace or tax base or job availability or *anything* important to the human environment. The ESA has no sense of balance, equity or conscience; it is committed only to protecting endangered species, no matter the cost, no matter how insignificant the return dividend might be.

So why *shouldn't* the Endangered Species Act be viewed with fear?

Hutchinson says the congressional "Declaration of Purposes and Policies" on the ESA spells it all out in a way that should not be feared at all: " . . . *encouraging the states and other interested parties through federal financial assistance, and a system of incentives, to develop and maintain conservation programs for endangered species.*"

Hutchinson adds, "I do not call confiscation of property, fines and other types of intimidation a 'system of incentives', nor do I call it 'financial assistance'."

And *that* is why the ESA is viewed with fear.

Hutchinson points out that the Fish and Wildlife Service has done many things contrary to what was intended—even to what was spelled out in official statements of policy. Again, the entire process shows the propensity of bureaucrats to act in the "public interest" for their own accretion of power and control.

III. **A Witch's Brew of Preservation Madness**

Ted Off and his family are dairy farmers in California's San Joaquin Valley. For more than five decades the Off family also raised most of the food supply for their cattle. As had been a customary practice for over half a century, Ted Off plowed a part of his acreage to prepare it for reseeding.

Without warning, the Off property was suddenly invaded by U.S. Fish and Wildlife Service officials and some employees of the California Department of Fish and Game— accompanied by an armed U.S. marshal. They served a warrant on the Offs, stating they had come to look for the remains of blunt-nosed leopard lizards in the cultivated field. For the better part of a day the federal officers swarmed over a 160-acre field, in vehicles and on foot.

They found no lizards nor body parts thereof.

Regardless, the Off family were still not out of the woods. They were informed by FWS agents that they had destroyed lizard habitat by plowing their field, and could still face federal criminal charges. Ted Off reasoned with officials that he had never seen a blunt-nosed lizard in 50 years of farming the land, and further, he had no idea he was doing anything wrong.

(If the FWS had interpreted what was *intended* by the ESA, then Ted Off *did* nothing wrong!)

To avoid prosecution for plowing a field that belonged to him, Off handed over the title to 60 acres of his land to the Fish and Wildlife Service—uncompensated!

(A man forced to surrender part of his property to stay out of jail is no different from the man who pays a ransom for the safe return of a loved one. They are both being "blackmailed" by someone capable of inflicting further harm upon them. Such behavior by a federal agency empowered to encourage conservation through assistance and incentives is akin to regulation mania.)

The Fish and Wildlife Service has demonstrated that it does not want cooperative efforts with private individuals; it only wants control—*full* control.

Beth Morian of Austin, Texas, discovered that nearly three dozen pairs of black-capped vireos were frequenting a part of her 1,300-acre ranch. The year was 1985, and the small birds were not yet listed as an endangered species. Morian, however, was a nature-lover and wildlife advocate who even served on the board of directors for the Zoological Society of Houston. She knew the black-capped vireos were thought to be declining in number, so she donated more than 60 acres of her property—land valued at nearly $2,000,000— as a natural preserve to be developed by the city of Austin.

The Morian family then proceeded with plans to develop and sell 66 home sites on a portion of their remaining acreage. They invested about $2,000,000 into the subdivision. The project was stopped in its tracks by a sudden FWS listing of the vireo as endangered. Development of the home sites was halted, and about half of the family's ranch was off limits to any activity that might disturb the birds.

Beth Morian could have cleared and developed her property without consequence had she done so quietly when she first noticed the vireos. A humanitarian gesture in the interest of preserving nature ultimately cost her the right to her land and the existence of her livelihood.

This is how the FWS would have it always.

Howard Hutchinson says, " . . . what we have taking place now are surrogate species . . . being petitioned onto the list with little scientific evidence to support their listings."

This means simply that some species are little more than "excuses" to tighten regulation, to restrict property rights, to broaden control of private land, to eliminate all forms of "public" activity on federally controlled lands. This behavior is not uncommon for federal agencies with no one overseeing them but the agencies themselves. There is no limit to the power they will grant themselves, and the acquired tolerance level of a civilized public allows them to exercise it. Out-of-control bureaucrats functioning unchecked within the bowels of controlling agencies do not recognize the existence of personal rights (property rights, constitutionally guaranteed civil rights, _any_ rights); they are very dangerous people because they are a serious threat to the very principles upon which this nation was founded.

A skeptic might say, "But we are only talking about protecting nature here."

_No!_

We are talking about _rights_—the right to privacy and the right of freedom to own land (something that is just now becoming a reality in some other parts of the world, but so taken for granted in this country that we are letting it slip away), the right to make wise choices in the pursuit of our own liberty and happiness and destiny.

We are talking about 1,600 acres of timber belonging to Ben Cone, near Greensboro, North Carolina, removed from any ownership or management authority of Cone (of course, he still pays the taxes) because red-cockaded woodpeckers are nesting there. Cone's wise management of the forest is what attracted the birds to begin with. In desperation, Cone clear-cut the rest of his property to prevent the government from taking control of it, too.

We are talking about 800 species of plants and animals on the endangered list in 1993, and another 3,300 under consideration. Every single species has the potential of curtailing the use of private land, idling economic development, stealing away dreams and rights and livelihoods. In the past, about 50 new species were added to the list each year. However, environmental groups sued the government to force a more rapid review process. In settlement of the suit FWS will examine 400 in three years, and hasten the review of 900 more.

We are talking about the Fish and Wildlife Service now considering *entire ecosystems* for listing, thereby avoiding the time-consuming review process for individual species as often as possible. The FWS has already drawn "biological" maps depicting the overlapping territories of goshawks and spotted owls, razorback suckers and bonytail chubs, and hundreds of other species spread across the land.

We are talking about the U.S. Fish and Wildlife Service, under authority of the Endangered Species Act, working very rapidly toward gaining control of all the land in this country.

IV. A Surprise Brought by Woodstorks

L.R. Goodson has raised cotton on his farm near Barwick, Georgia, for nearly half a century. Weather and insects and increasing regulation have never allowed his to become an easy job, but it is his "way of life." He even instilled in his daughter Betty a sense of pride in the "farmer's ethic," and she became a partner in his work.

In late 1992, the Goodsons hardly noticed a road-widening project going on halfway across Brooks County. And they could not have imagined how the project would affect them.

Betty Goodson West answered her phone one day and was told that a wetlands mitigation plan was underway, and she and her father were in the middle of it. It seems the Georgia Department of Transportation had disturbed some habitat of the endangered woodstork while working on U.S. 84 near Thomasville. In order to fix the problem, they had decided to build a new habitat for the birds on Goodson's property.

The Georgia DOT had selected a 40-acre site in the middle of a 300-acre cotton field!

West told the DOT official on the phone that the property was not for sale at any price. Very soon a letter came from the district engineer, explaining that state law requires the creation of new habitat if existing critical habitat has been destroyed or altered. The same law would allow the DOT to begin surveying the Goodson property.

Three truckloads of surveyors showed up in February of 1993—just as Goodson was preparing his field for planting—and went to work, positioning transits and pulling lines. While there _is_ a cypress swamp not far from the property, the cottonfield had never been classified as wetland. A single drainage ditch has sliced through the property for more than 70 years.

DOT engineers also determined they would have to build a 60-foot access road across the farm to the newly-constructed woodstork sanctuary.

Brewer Pope, a friend and neighbor of L.R. Goodson, organized a grassroots protest of the incident, collecting hundreds of signatures from disbelieving Georgians on a petition aimed at the DOT. Meanwhile, single-minded state and federal officials continued to function under authority of a state law that effectively gives them power to "take" Goodson's land.

This story is just one of hundreds that illustrate why the Endangered Species Act of 1973 is a nightmare for property-owning Americans. And it again poses the question: Is the ESA serving to accomplish what lawmakers intended (or envisioned) when they enacted it?

Congress recognized more than two decades ago that economic growth and development had rendered various species of fish, wildlife and plants extinct, and they realized that some other species were threatened with a similar fate—species declared to have " . . . _aesthetic, ecological, educational, historical, recreational, and scientific value to the Nation and its people._" The U.S. committed then (with passage of and language written into the ESA) to conserving various species " . . . _to the extent practicable._"

Black's Law Dictionary defines "practicable" as "that which may be done, practiced, or accomplished; that which is performable, feasible, possible . . . " On that basis alone, acts that deprive people of life, liberty or property, or acts that imperil traditions, cultures and economies (all protected by the Constitution), are not *practicable*.

The Fish and Wildlife Service is clearly not meeting the goals or satisfying the intentions of Congress in 1973. The agency bureaucrats are simply tending to their own agendas.

Other provisions of the Endangered Species Act direct that " . . . *Federal agencies shall cooperate with State and local agencies*" (as amended in 1982), and command the Secretary to consider " . . . *economic impact, and any other relevant impact*" when addressing threatened or endangered species, water resource issues and critical habitat.

None of them does any of this. As stated by Brewer Pope in the case of L.R. Goodson's cottonfield, "This is . . . simply 'taking' private property at the whim of two or three bureaucrats somewhere."

In self-defense, frightened property owners often *destroy* certain species before the consequences of their presence are incurred. While the ESA is not a bad law in the way it was intended, it is having a negative effect in some cases as a direct result of the way it is being enforced.

An act of Congress is worthless (even detrimental) without proper implementation. The Endangered Species Act was once touted as the "crown jewel" of sensible environmental legislation. Twenty years later, it is a blight— a cancer—helping to rapidly destroy remaining vestiges of the American Dream. It is a law gone bad, a worthy effort turned ugly by zealots who want only to control. Lawmakers who helped craft the innovative legislation now try to distance themselves from it.

Empowered by the ESA, the U.S. Fish and Wildlife Service has reached a pinnacle of achievement in the abuse of federal agency powers. FWS agents have long forgotten their roles as public servants; they now function as masters of a kingdom—the kingdom of animals to which all of humankind is becoming subservient, like it or not.

The Endangered Species Act, as intended and written, could work to the benefit of all; there would be little argument or opposition from landowners, or anyone else, if that were the case. There would, in fact, be financial assistance and a system of incentives. There would be cooperation and interaction between federal agencies and other interested parties. Sensible and intelligent determinations would be based on scientific data and other pertinent information. Landowners, regulating agencies and the species themselves would live and function in concert with a diverse and adaptable environment.

Too few bureaucrats with too much power and too little supervision have forsaken this ideal. They meet sincere interest from outside groups and individuals with argument, arrogance and patronization. They excel in bureaucratic repugnance, freely apply government force and coercion, and create population displacement and economic devastation.

They destroy the private lives and livelihoods of citizens of the United States of America.

V. An Environmental Feeding Frenzy

In a single magnanimous gesture meant to smooth the feathers of Fund for Animals in 1992, President Bush made a grave mistake (with regard to property owners and other lands users) when he directed government lawyers to "settle" a stubborn lawsuit. Terms of the settlement included doubling (perhaps tripling) the number of so-called "endangered" or "threatened" species within a very short period of time, as well as speeding the review process for thousands of candidate species.

This was perceived by preservationists as a carte blanche blessing for thousands of ambitious crusaders to emerge from the woodwork, each with a driving desire to "save" some creature. In March of 1992, campaigns for listing 7,202 different species as threatened or endangered had already been launched within the 50 states. There were 1,024 different proposals in California, 245 in Oregon, 306 in Texas, 226 in North Carolina, 92 in Illinois, and similar numbers, higher and lower, tallied from every state. More than half of the candidates for listing are invertebrates—slugs, spiders and beetles, including one species of cockroach—and more than a third are rodents.

Early in 1993, Interior Secretary Bruce Babbitt said his *foremost goal* was to protect the diversity of plant and animal life in the United States through the Endangered Species Act. He might as well have thrown a live dog to a school of piranhas. Since then, the environmental waters have teamed with voracious preservation radicals who cannot strip the flesh of property rights fast enough from the skeletons of private landowners and traditional users of government-controlled lands.

Three species of protected salmon have crippled the fishing industry and hydroelectric power supply on the Snake and Columbia Rivers. The listings of the Bruneau hot springs snail and five other mollusks have idled farmers and ranchers in southwestern Idaho. A blind salamander threatens to curtail the water supply for the city of San Antonio, Texas. The Delhi sands fly has blocked redevelopment of a closed military base in southern California. Protection of the desert tortoise has effectively removed ranchers and recreationists alike from millions of acres in the desert Southwest. Spotted owls have eliminated tens of thousands of taxpayers from the workforce throughout the northern and western states. Protected rats and lizards in California have forced farmers to leave their tractors in their barns. Human activity is not permitted within a mile of denning wolves in parts of Wyoming. Irrigation water is withheld from Oregon farmers so the public can better "appreciate" two species of suckerfish.

The list of incredible consequences resulting from enforcement of the Endangered Species Act is virtually endless. And yet Secretary Babbitt has stated, "My feeling is that the Endangered Species Act has not been used in a pro-active way. The one lesson you can see from the last ten years is, you can't use it passively."

(What the *hell* is he talking about!)

The definition of "passive," according to *Webster's New World Dictionary*, is " . . . inactive, but acted upon."

Many tens of thousands of victimized Americans, having felt the brunt of the ESA, would call it anything but "inactive."

Fueled by Babbitt's anti-people mentality, preservationists and eco-bureaucrats are having a field day—all at the expense of landowners, developers, working Americans, entire industries, municipalities and their economies. Additionally, taxpayer dollars are utilized to _study_ candidate species for possible listing, as demonstrated by researchers at Oregon State University compiling a "status report" on the Fender's blue butterfly for consideration by the Fish and Wildlife Service. Three Audubon Society chapters sued the FWS to force a rapid listing of the western snowy plover. Federal tax dollars paid for courtroom proceedings. _Anyone_ can apply for the listing of a species, and _anyone_ can sue to expedite the process. These are not uncommon practices.

Each species designated as threatened or endangered is entitled, under a supreme court ruling, to _full protection regardless of the cost!_ Some environmental analysts have predicted the price of enforcing the ESA will make the taxpayer bailout of the collapsed savings-and-loan industry look like small potatoes.

Still, the mad assault continues, and plans get bolder.

Fish and Wildlife officials revealed in 1993 their desire to designate 2,094 miles of the Colorado River and its tributaries as "critical habitat" for the razorback sucker, the Colorado squawfish, and the bonytail and humpback chubs—four species of trash fish listed as endangered. A "biological support" document, prepared by FWS biologists, outlined the biological importance of the rivers with respect to protecting the fish. Thousands of farmers and ranchers, landowners, industries and municipalities across Utah, Colorado, New Mexico, Arizona, Nevada and California, rose up in opposition to the proposal, but were summarily ignored. The "final rule" affecting 1,980 miles of the original proposed area was published in _The Federal Register_ in March, 1994. An official news release from FWS stated: " . . . no areas were excluded from the proposed designation based upon economic or other relevant impacts . . . "

"Economic or other relevant impacts" were never a consideration because FWS is not charged with preserving anything concerning humans. There is a tremendous "biological importance" attached to those life-giving rivers and streams of the arid Southwest by the human element who depends on them for survival. However, as in this case, government agencies prefer to move quietly when pursing ambiguous goals; they don't want to be discovered. They conduct poorly publicized public meetings on short notice in difficult locations. Their rhetoric is refined to make even the most ruthless scheme appear innocuous (even beneficial). They reassure landowners and the public (verbally) that no "significant changes" will result from their actions.

It is all a part of the process of taking control. It's about now in that process that audiences would do well to recall Michael Rowe, the California rancher who discovered too late his ranch had been consumed by a kangaroo rat "study area" and was denied the right to build a house.

Anyone who believes agriculture and industry, tourism and other river access will not be affected by the critical habitat designation for the razorback sucker and other species on the Colorado and its tributaries should go back to sleep because their dream is not over. At the end of 1993, the stream-fed municipal water supply to 10,000 residents of Graham County, Arizona, had already been severed while the "study" was ongoing, and local governments were resorting to groundwells for residential water.

The Endangered Species Act is a federal law which supports halting any and all activity that might endanger a wildlife species. There is no provision for human welfare in this law. And there is no species allowed to be judged more important or significant than another. As it is perversely interpreted and executed, the ESA guarantees broader rights and protection to snails, insects and crustaceans than to humans.

Not surprisingly, it's mostly rural America that endures the toughest assault. That's because rural America encompasses the lands, assets and resources most coveted by environmental extremists and control-mad bureaucrats. Rural Americans engage in the kinds of activities that cause eco-salvationists to have nightmares—activities like producing food and clothing and lumber, extracting fuels and minerals from the earth, and pursuing honest livelihoods in concert with nature.

One year into the Clinton Presidency, the really big guns were just being assembled for a full-scale offensive against property owners and their rights.

Secretary Babbitt, disenchanted with the tedious process of listing single species, has devised what he calls the "multi-species ecosystem approach."

(Are you scared yet?)

The Secretary believes he needs "more flexibility" in administering and enforcing the Endangered Species Act. His plan is to bypass the perplexing procedures of scientifically documenting the requirements for listing each and every species. He wants simply to _list ecosystems_ with hundreds of species included. An assistant to Babbitt defines an "ecosystem" as " . . . an area as small as an acre . . . or . . . such as Yellowstone National Park."

Babbitt says simply that an ecosystem "is in the eye of the beholder."

(Do you see how much flexibility the Secretary wants?)

Powercrats like Babbitt don't deal well with the realization that 60 percent of America's ecosystems are located on private land. He has spoken of "discarding the concept of property and trying to find a different understanding of natural landscape." He wants to eradicate "the individualistic view of property" and implement a "communitarian interpretation." He says, "You can't build fences around property."

The "different understanding" Babbitt envisions is an "understanding" among Americans that _he_ controls it all. He is cleverly and quickly moving in that direction. His secret weapon (and the biggest gun of the arsenal) is the National Biological Survey.

This $180,000,000 Babbitt brainchild will give the Secretary almost everything he wants. When this newest agency of the Interior Department (NBS) is approved by Congress, land use rights (private and otherwise) will exist only at the pleasure of the Secretary and his army of eco-crats.

The National Biological Survey, under the direction of Babbitt, will be charged with mapping and cataloging everything that "walks, crawls, swims or flies" in this country. There will be no boundaries the government researchers can't cross—including private fences and "No Trespassing" signs! And, as if that weren't enough flexibility for the Secretary, the NBS legislation waives compliance with the Freedom of Information Act. This means quite simply property owners will *not have access* to the biological data gathered on their own properties! They will not be allowed to challenge a determination or a regulation or a restriction in the use of their properties.

At least the ESA allows for challenges and reviews, and even applications for *de*listings. Under the NBS, there is no way to identify the enemy. Babbitt would rather take control of private property and eliminate activity on federally-managed lands by claiming protection of a "fragile ecosystem" than to name an insect or mollusk as his ally.

Either way, property rights and basic human rights are in big trouble. The creation of the National Biological Survey, and implementation of "ecosystem management," will provide radical environmentalists and control-driven bureaucrats the firepower they need for total annihilation of the American way of life.

VI. The Insignificance of Man

One snowy night in September of 1989, John Shuler of Dupuyer, Montana, woke to a commotion in his sheep pen. He grabbed a rifle and went to investigate. Three grizzly bears were killing Shuler's sheep. Shuler fired shots into the night air to frighten them away. Sensing movement behind him, he turned quickly to face a large grizzly rearing up to attack. He shot the bear and ran for the safety of his ranchhouse.

The next morning Shuler went to examine the carcass of the bear he thought he'd killed. The grizzly was there, all right, but alive and angry. The animal charged, and John Shuler shot it dead. Shuler reported the incident and was told he would be prosecuted for killing an endangered species.

Trial convened in federal court in Great Falls. Represented by William Perry Pendley of the Mountain States Legal Foundation, Shuler claimed self-defense.

After hearing two days of argument from Pendley and government lawyers, the federal administrative law judge ruled in order to assert the "self-defense" exception of the Endangered Species Act a defendant must pass the same "test" used in criminal law when one human being has killed another in the course of claimed self-protection.

In criminal law, self-defense in not a valid claim if the defendant is "blameworthy to some degree in bringing about the occasion for the need to use deadly force." Neither is self-defense acceptable under the law if the defendant "provokes an encounter as a result of which he finds it necessary to use deadly force to defend himself."

The judge applied both circumstances to Shuler.

(Folks, we are talking about the killing of a _bear!_)

The judge said when Shuler left his house to protect his sheep, he "purposefully" entered into a "zone of imminent danger of a bear attack." Shuler's self-defense claim was denied. He was found guilty and ordered to pay a $4,000 civil penalty.

The judge said Shuler (or anyone living and working in grizzly country) had two choices before leaving his house. He could have left his livestock (and livelihood) to the mercy of predators, or he could have gone to their aid without a deadly weapon.

Neither option is reasonable.

The legal opinion rendered in this case was unprecedented and ludicrous. However, it bears out a growing sentiment among animal rights fanatics and eco-preservation radicals that human life form is meant to take a back seat to most other animals (and some plants, too) in the natural scheme of nature's processes.

David Graber, a biologist with the National Park Service, contends that those with a true allegiance to nature can only "hope for the right virus to come along."

Dave Foreman, founder of the militant environmentalist group Earth First!, has advocated, "Move out the people and cars . . . reclaim the roads and plowed lands."

Paul Watson, founder of Greenpeace, calls the human species "the AIDS of the earth."

Philosophy professor Paul Taylor said the "demise of the human species would be no loss."

Edward Abbey, author of *Desert Solitaire*, stated openly, "I would rather kill a man than a snake."

A worrisome thing about this twisted mind-set is that a faction of the element is writing curriculum for impressionable children in the public schools. Nearly three dozen states have formal "environmental education" curricula in place, and it's not uncommon to find the study material originating out of the Sierra Club or other single-sighted preservationist group.

The programs do not teach socioeconomics. They do not address history, tradition or social human culture. They avoid the political theorem upon which our young nation was founded. They claim to teach ecology while their textbooks are saturated with propaganda and untruths.

One such manual claims "people are responsible for causing the extinction of 10,000 species a year." Researchers for the International Union for the Conservation of Nature, however, say the rate for birds and mammals is closer to one species a year.

A textbook used at junior high grade levels declares that global warming is causing the world's food supply to dwindle away, and that "entire islands (are) disappearing under rising seas." Ronald Bailey, an associate at the Competitive Enterprise Institute in Washington, D.C., and author of the meticulously documented *EcoScam: The False Prophets of Ecological Apocalypse*, says, "There is *no* upward trend in the globe's temperature. For the past 14 years it has been essentially stable. Global warming is another myth."

Eco-alarmists need frightening myths and orchestrated predictions of doom to perpetuate their causes. Bailey goes on to describe a "strong anti-capitalist thread in the environmental movement." He says a great many environmental activists are alienated from the modern technical capitalist U.S. society, and "hope to return us to a more primitive communitarian lifestyle."

(Didn't we hear Bruce Babbitt say something about "communitarian interpretation?")

Alston Chase, syndicated columnist and author of _Playing God In Yellowstone: The Destruction of America's First National Park,_ writes, "Educators promote these lies because their aim is not encouraging reflection (on human interaction with ecology) but manipulating children for political agendas."

School-aged children have no defense against this approach. They have no reason to be suspect of material presented in the classroom. If an instructor or textbook says Thomas Jefferson wrote the Declaration of Independence, then it must be true. Why would a course on the environment be any less credible?

In 1992, the Turner Broadcasting System distributed to schools propaganda packets, each one labeled "Save the Earth Action Pack." Kids were told to pledge more "time and money" to environmental lobbyists.

Radical eco-preservationists have found a way to undermine the very fundamental basis of this nation— through its children. Educators are allowing it to happen because they are either not knowledgeable on the subject, they themselves have been fooled, or they support the movement.

Any parent who owns property, pays taxes, enjoys the availability and use of unappropriated lands, or believes in the principles of freedom outlined by our founding fathers, should examine the environmental agenda of the local public schools.

Eco-radicals are bothered by the western system of democratic politics. They defy the American concept that free people should be allowed to look out for themselves, to make decisions, to manage their own affairs, use the land and prosper from it, determine their own destinies. Some of the more ambitious ones have maneuvered themselves into key positions within the very government they seek to weaken.

They do not believe in property rights or personal freedoms. They believe in centralized control of the human race. They favor multinational organizations beyond the reach of voter sentiment—organizations like the United Nation's Commission on Environment and Development, or perhaps Earth Summit.

(DOI Secretary Bruce Babbitt serves as Natural Resources Secretary with the Tri-Lateral Commission—a coalition of political interests from the U.S., Western Europe and Japan.)

They will have the people of the world subservient to all the animal kingdom of the world before they cease their battle. In recruiting the children as their allies, they dramatically increase their chances of unqualified victory.

VII. **The Environmental Vortex**

The Endangered Species Act is clearly a law gone bad. It allows for (even encourages) almost indiscriminate abuse of power and authority. It has become a tool used broadly by control-mad regulators who wish only to eliminate all resistance, and by preservation extremists who would impose upon all mankind a second-class existence to serve the greater needs of insects, worms and weeds.

In many cases (as mentioned earlier by Howard Hutchinson), "surrogate" species are often listed in order to "protect" something else. Opponents to a multi-million-dollar international observatory on a remote mountaintop in southern Arizona used a subspecies of red squirrel to try to block the project (the whole story in Part Three). Conservation radicals worried about old-growth forests being logged have tied their opposition efforts to several available species of owl—northern spotted, California spotted or Mexican spotted—depending on the locations of the forests.

As it turns out, the less known about a particular "subspecies" of squirrel, owl or other type of animal, the easier and quicker it seems to receive special consideration—over all consideration for the _human_ environment. As environmental zealots apply additional pressure to Fish and Wildlife officials to begin reviewing and _listing_ entire ecosystems as threatened or endangered, there will be no consideration for whose private property might lay within the ecosystem, nor for the renewable resources or economies or cultures existing there.

Laws like the ESA occasionally come up for congressional review; however, that very agenda was set aside in 1992 because no one wanted to get near it during an election year. Another year passed in 1993 without any attempt to restructure the controversial legislation. Sadly, even laws gone bad are seldom repaired and virtually never repealed. Lobbyists paid by the Sierra Club and dozens of other groups swarm to Capitol Hill like bees around a kicked hive when the topic comes up. They are horrified at the prospect of losing control of land and lives across America, and doubly so at any mention of having to curtail their push to control it all.

The laws then become even more restrictive. The agencies assume broader powers. And rarely does anyone fight back because we Americans are civilized.

(We've learned not to resist those we perceive as more powerful, remember?)

We will resist resisting and tolerate the intolerable until we have lost everything to them—our property, our rights, our freedoms and destinies—like possessions sucked into a whirlpool. Then it will be too late. You cannot escape the deadly vortex after it pulls you under.

Former Governor of Washington Dixy Lee Ray said, "The Endangered Species Act is broke." She went on, "Not the intelligent community nor the scientific community nor any community in this country is organized sufficiently . . . to prevent reenactment of the ESA as it is . . . or perhaps even worse."

Ray believed those most actively involved in the ever-spreading environmental movement have a general plan for changing the way life is lived in the western world. She said they truly believe in centralized government, and they scoff at the sovereignty of the people of the United States. "They would have us give up our own nation to come under . . . a single world government . . . "

The time to resist is *before* the whirlpool sucks you in.

VIII. **An Argument for Delisting**

Everyone knows the timber industry has been nearly halted in this country by the various listings of spotted owls as either threatened or endangered. In the Pacific Northwest and other locations across the northern tier states, it's the northern spotted owl (more on this in Part Four). In northern California, it's a close cousin—the California spotted owl. In Arizona, Colorado and New Mexico, where logging has never been competitive with the Northwest (but has sustained numerous localized economies), it's the Mexican spotted owl.

Even without the benefit of solid scientific data, the Mexican spotted owl is listed as "threatened" by the Fish and Wildlife Service. For all intents and purposes, the U.S. Forest Service has managed timberlands (and timber sales) in the Southwest since 1989 just as if the subspecies were endangered.

Economic backlash only promises to worsen.

As of mid-1993, sawmill operations in Arizona required an inflow of 235,000,000 board feet just to stay alive. Under tightening regulation by the Clinton Administration, the industry will be allowed an annual harvest of only 100,000,000 board feet. Entire communities with no other industry (like Heber and Eager) will become ghost towns born of the '90s.

(Where is the preservation of culture, as guaranteed in the Constitution?)

Before the listing of the Mexican spotted owl, more than a dozen independent timber contractors were providing jobs for hundreds of families in northern Arizona and contributing millions of dollars to various local economies. In mid-1993, only one remained, and its future was questionable.

In glaring irony to all this, a 1993 report from the Forest Service shows that the Southwest still contains as many old-growth trees in its national forests as it did 30 years ago, and this does not include designated wilderness areas where logging is prohibited altogether. The report goes on to say that forested land in Arizona and New Mexico has *increased* since 1962. Restricted logging and effective fire suppression are factors largely responsible for tree density in some areas so heavy that disease and insects have had debilitating effects.

Quoting from the official Forest Service report: "...some assert that the Southwest has been logged over and that the timber industry faces a rapid decline because of over-logging. This is simply not true."

There once were two industries in Catron County, New Mexico. Prior to 1989, ranching contributed $21,000,000 to the local economy, and the timber industry spent almost $7,000,000. Following implementation of Mexican spotted owl "interim guidelines," the Stone Container Reserve Sawmill dropped to one shift, and financial input decreased accordingly—by half. In March of 1993, the mill closed indefinitely for lack of available timber, and one-fourth of the Catron County economy was dead.

Howard Hutchinson of the Coalition of Arizona/New Mexico Counties says, "Families are being ripped apart in order to survive—breadwinners are being forced to go to Colorado, Alaska and elsewhere, just to work."

(What happened to the value of the family unit, as perceived by the founders of a nation based on strength through solidarity? Have we truly become a land of subjects serving animals?)

The Fish and Wildlife Service, the Sierra Club and many dozens more agencies and organizations would have us accept that. And with the help of numerous radical preservationists wrought with a desire for central control (not excluding DOI Secretary Bruce Babbitt, Vice President Al Gore and President Bill Clinton), we will see complete materialization of that civil rights-quashing, freedom-strangling nightmare if no one resists.

Occasionally, a group or individual, a local government entity, a concerned organization or coalition, will take the owl by the horns, so to speak, and file a protest or lawsuit, list an objection, or even request the "delisting" of a species. Such was the case when the Coalition of Arizona/New Mexico Counties filed for delisting of the Mexican spotted owl in August, 1993.

The process for delisting a species is much the same as for listing a species, except for one basic difference—it takes longer because it's like driving your car home in reverse. However, a petition for delisting *any* species may be submitted to the Fish and Wildlife Service, and the agency *must* consider it. Of course, there are no guarantees that any species will be delisted, by petition or otherwise, but sometimes the evidence presented in favor of delisting (as in the case of the Mexican spotted owl) is overwhelming.

(The findings within this petition are in themselves an illustration of the covert workings of the FWS and the ESA, and reason enough that the agency *and* the law should both be feared.)

The Mexican spotted owl (MSO) delisting petition submitted to John Rogers, Regional Director of the USFWS in Albuquerque, states: "Due to the preponderance of the evidence cited . . . and now following, there does not appear to be any present or threatened destruction, modification, or curtailment of the MSO's habitat or range other than the failure to manage the density and fuel loading in the southwestern forests."

(This simply means that thinning of the forests through managed logging would be of substantial benefit to MSO habitat.)

The delisting petition continues:

"1) The only conclusions a reasonable person can discern from current data is that:

"a) High MSO population densities occur in secondary growth forests . . . " (this from Forest Service inventories on the Lincoln and Gila National Forests every year from 1988 through 1992. Remember, the MSO listing has blocked timber harvest in _old-growth_ forests.)

"b) The dominant characteristic of MSO habitat is steep narrow canyons . . . " (from numerous studies, 1977 through 1993, USFS update reports, and publications in _The Federal Register Notice_. Again, not old-growth forests.)

"c) The MSO does not have the same habitat requirements of the northern or California spotted owls. . . " (as supported by accredited scientific data. Conjecture to the contrary was included in the petition for listing the MSO.)

"e) Nearly all habitat is either intact or has increased since the 1930s . . . " (from Forest Service data. Of course, the opposite was purported as truth in the listing process.)

"l) Little, if any, consideration is given to the millions of acres of wilderness and de facto wilderness throughout the owl's range;

"m) The FWS's analysis of data has been biased due to most inventories having been conducted on proposed or active timber sale lands;

"n) No significant inventories have been conducted in middle or low elevation riparian areas to determine occupancy . . . "

The last three issues point sharply to the fact that the data "collected" and submitted for listing of the MSO was tainted by biases and deliberate efforts to curtail timber harvest—a classic example of the "surrogate species" used deceptively to achieve an entirely different end.

The petition for delisting the Mexican spotted owl is 19 single-spaced, elite-type pages of similar evidence (all well-researched and documented) which shine a glaring light on the conspiratorial behavior of one federal agency (FWS) in bed with radical preservationists and advocates of centralized control.

The MSO listing—based on flawed data, creative speculation, admitted survey bias and juxtaposition of information on other owl species—has cost families their livelihoods, southwestern communities their economies, an industry its lifeblood, and millions of dollars in lost federal revenues.

Eco-bureaucrats, preservation extremists and noetic cultists do not care. It is simply one more step in their plan for a new way of life within their envisioned Utopian Western World. Therefore, it came as no big surprise to anyone on April 1, 1994, when the Fish and Wildlife Service denied the Coalition of Arizona/New Mexico Counties' petition for delisting the Mexican spotted owl. Their reason: " . . . the petition . . . did not present substantial information indicating delisting . . . warranted."

As stated before, delisting a species is a long and doubtful process. Nonetheless, delisting petitions do get filed—mostly in defense of property rights and jobs, lifestyles and economies. Efforts have been started to delist the California spotted owl where thousands of jobs are at stake.

There are many others. However, the preservationists are "dug in" on all fronts, ready to defend each and every listing, not unlike mothers defending their babies.

After a petition for delisting is submitted to the USFWS, the agency has three months to determine whether the request is warranted. Consideration for the human environment is not a part of the process. If the request is found to have merit, at best, a Status Review Team of biologists (good luck!) has a year to ponder the case while public hearings are held (if you're lucky). Meanwhile, property and homes and jobs and businesses and economies succumb to the prolonged stranglehold.

Preservation fanatics will not rest until every species on earth is somehow listed for protection. This drive, however, is not aimed at protecting the animals from anything so much as it is orchestrated to control the land and regulate the movement (restrict the freedom) of people upon it.

(This is where tolerant Americans should begin to resist.)

The Oregon Natural Resources Council is fighting for the listing of 83 types of snails and clams as endangered species. Farming, ranching, the timber and mining industries, as well as other industry and recreation will be seriously affected by a "critical habitat" designation for "endangered" trash fish in six western states. A professor at the University of California at Riverside boasts on national television that "his" listing of the Delhi sands fly (cousin to the housefly) successfully stopped a $10,000,000 development.

A draft recovery plan for the desert tortoise, issued by Fish and Wildlife as mandated by the ESA, affects nearly 4,800,000 acres of land in California, over 1,300,000 acres in Nevada, almost 500,000 acres in Arizona, and 137,000 acres in Utah. That's more than 6,600,000 total acres in four states! The final critical habitat for the desert tortoise, as laid out in the FWS Recovery Plan, will allow no livestock grazing, and such activities as mining, rockhounding, off-roading, will all cease to occur. All access to the acreage will be severely restricted—and these restrictions will be in place _forever!_

(Don't think for a minute that the next listing, critical habitat determination, crippling restrictions, loss of rights, liberty, pursuit of happiness and livelihood, might not occur in _your own back yard._)

No one, nothing, nowhere, is off-limits to the preservation extremists who work tirelessly for total control of everyone, everything, everywhere.

III.

A SAGA
OF
SQUIRRELS
AND
TELESCOPES

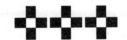

I. **In the Beginning**

(This complex story must be told in its entirety, for nowhere is there a clearer picture of radical preservationists attempting to smother development—*any kind* of development—to foster their own noetic obsession.)

In 1846, Lt. William Emory, a topographical engineer, named the highest mountain in the Pinaleno (Peen-uh-layn'-yoh) Range after his senior officer, Lt. Col. William Duncan Graham. Emory, at the time, was on a mapping expedition of the rugged mountain chain in southeastern Arizona.

Mt. Graham rises to 10,720 feet very near the center of the magnificent 300-square-mile Pinalenos. Today, it is referred to as a "sky island," jutting intrepidly upward from the arid desert floor.

A flurry of historical development and other activity occurred on Mt. Graham and throughout the mother range during the late 1800s. Outlaws hid there, as did Apache renegades running away from the San Carlos Indian Reservation. Native coniferous forests were harvested by undauntable pioneer loggers. Several sawmills flourished, producing lumber for the lowland communities developing in the Sulphur Springs Valley to the south and along the Gila River to the north. A ten-mile-long flume carried green-sawed lumber from the mountain to the valley floor near Smithville (now Pima). Mexican *banditos* are said to have buried stolen gold and silver there. Gen. Nelson Miles used Mt. Graham as one of 14 heliograph stations sending Morse code messages from mountain to mountain, all the way to Mexico, trying to capture the elusive Geronimo.

Today's visitor travels State Route 366 to designated camping and picnicking areas like Treasure Park, Soldier Creek and Riggs Flat Lake. The roadway ascends through five distinctive ecological planes in a span of 20 miles, traversing desert greasewoods and prickly pears, scrub oaks and alligator junipers, manzanita groves and lush mountain forest commingling evergreens and aspens.

In the early 1980s, Mt. Graham became the focal point for a new community of explorers. Astronomers on the cutting edge of space research found themselves faced with too many important projects and too little time available on large telescopes within the United States. They began searching for a new site for the "next generation" of ground-based observing instruments.

The University of Arizona (renowned for its astronomy program), the Vatican Observatory in Italy, the Max Planck Institute of Germany, and others, became partners in the plan. They studied 280 mountaintops above 9,000 feet elevation, rating them all on altitude, low humidity, absence of cloud cover, absence of light pollution, and proximity to an existing astronomical facility.

The astronomers selected Mt. Graham, sharing many unique characteristics with other potential sites, but also boasting a paved state highway almost to its summit and many other signs of previous development. Heliograph Peak contained several commercial electronics towers and a lookout for fire patrol. A variety of recreational opportunities—campsites, picnic grounds, hiking trails, horse corrals, private summer cabins, a church camp and two manmade lakes for fishing. About 10,000 acres in the range had been logged and reforested in the last six decades.

In 1984, Congress passed the Arizona Wilderness Act, which designated 3,500 acres as a potential astrophysical research study area (remember that acreage figure) in the Pinaleno Mountains. At the same time the range was designated as a federal wilderness study area.

University scientists then began working with federal and state agencies to prepare two biological assessments (by the U.S. Forest Service), two biological opinions (by the U.S. Fish and Wildlife Service), an environmental impact statement, and to conduct numerous public hearings and public comment periods. University public relations officials wrote letters of intent to the various Native American tribes throughout the Southwest, requesting their opinion on the proposed observatory project.

Overall, the preliminary work took four years.

The attention to detail in all the studies, public meetings and correspondence was to minimize the impact of such a project on the Mt. Graham environment and the people with close ties to it. When the residents of Graham County learned they would never see hulking telescope domes looming on the Mt. Graham horizon, and that placing scopes there would not terminate public access to "their mountain," they became overwhelmingly supportive. No response—negative or positive—was received during this period from any of the Native American groups.

II. **Enter the Red Squirrel**

(Rest assured that no development on public land— or *private*—is immune to fatalistic scrutiny by ever-vigilant preservationists.)

Lo and behold, a rare squirrel lives on Mt. Graham!

It's the same squirrel that's been there for centuries (although a few Graham County old-timers recall importing some from Texas). It's not very big and it's red, and it behaves much the same as other red squirrels located in the White Mountains of Arizona, the Kaibab National Forest, and other parts of North America. It's the same squirrel listed by the Arizona Game and Fish Department as an authorized game animal until 1986.

At the urging of Dr. Robin Silver, a Phoenix-based eco-preservationist and wildlife photographer, the Fish and Wildlife Service listed the "unique subspecies" as endangered in 1987.

Biologists agreed rather summarily that thousands of years of isolation at the higher altitudes of the Pinaleno Mountains probably caused a slight genetic difference in this squirrel. One researcher wrote in the *Tucson Daily Star* that the squirrel possesses an allele—the same genetic phenomenon that causes appaloosas to bear spots and Australian shepherds to have white eyes, but he did not know what *this* allele does.

The entire scope of the observatory project began to rapidly change with the rather hurried listing of the Mt. Graham red squirrel (*Tamiasciurus Hudsonicus Grahamensis*).

The University of Arizona cut its plan for 18 telescopes to seven, confined to two peaks. University planners and federal agents agreed in 1988 that the observatory would be limited to *one* peak, and built in two stages. The cost was estimated then at $200,000,000.

A 1,700-acre area surrounding the observatory site on Emerald Peak was designated as a refugium area for the sole protection of the rodent subspecies, off-limits to anyone not in possession of a Forest Service permit.

Congress enacted the Arizona-Idaho Conservation Act of 1988, incorporating the terms of the U.S. Fish and Wildlife Service Biological Opinion, agreed to by the Forest Service and the University. The law authorized the University and its partners to build *three* telescopes and an access road on Emerald Peak as the first phase of the observatory. If a biological study by the Fish and Wildlife Service showed no serious impact on the red squirrels after completion of the first three scopes, then four more telescopes (the second phase) could be built, so long as the entire seven-instrument observatory, all its support facilities and roads occupied no more than 24 acres.

Let's back up for a moment, though, and consider some requirements of the law (as demanded by the FWS, preservation extremists and militant environmentalists).

The first stage of the project (expected to cost upwards of $80,000,000) could involve only three telescopes and a *new* two-mile-long access road. An *existing* five-mile-long access road was to be closed and restored (reforested) to its natural state. Hundreds of spruce and Douglas fir trees were transplanted from the new road site to the old one.

(Many stipulations in the federal mandate seemed to be tailored to make the observatory project more difficult, rather than more feasible or logical.)

The total area occupied by the first three telescopes and the access road could not exceed 8.6 acres. The road itself would consume more than six of those acres. Individually, one scope would sit on a one-fourth-acre site, another would take up one-third of an acre, and the third instrument would occupy 1.2 acres. These tiny areas of development within 11,000-plus acres of recognized suitable red squirrel habitat would equate roughly to dropping a couple of pennies and a nickel in the middle of an average-sized livingroom floor. (Remember the original study area was 3,500 acres?)

The legislation also required the University to spend at least $100,000 a year for a minimum of 10 years to monitor the impact of telescope construction on the endangered Mt. Graham red squirrel. University expenditures for the monitoring program have averaged more than $200,000 per year in the years since its implementation.

The University and its partners complied with every stipulation within the federal law, and construction began at the site of the first telescope in late spring of 1989.

That summer, the Sierra Club Legal Defense Fund filed a nine-claim lawsuit against the Forest Service and the Fish and Wildlife Service. It named the red squirrel as a plaintiff. Contention among Sierra Club activists and other opponents of the telescopes was that construction of an observatory would lead to disruption of the red squirrel habitat and ultimate extinction of the subspecies.

The University intervened in the suit as a co-defendant, then, because it was obvious that stopping the telescope project was the real intent of the litigation. After three years of court battles—motions, objections, depositions, oral arguments, rulings and appeals, during which work on the observatory proceeded only sporadically—the Ninth U.S. Circuit Court of Appeals upheld the original rulings of a federal judge in Tucson, and threw out all nine claims.

During these years of ongoing legal proceedings and construction activities, biologists charged with monitoring the red squirrels saw an _increase_ in their population from as few as 116 squirrels in the spring of 1989 to as many as 385 in the fall of 1993. These same observers also reported that the majority of the "unique subspecies" were actually living in lower altitudes of the mixed conifer zone.

(Obviously, establishment of the 1,700-acre protective refugium was based on inaccurate information that Mt. Graham red squirrels required higher-elevation spruce-fir habitat.)

As of late 1993, the Fish and Wildlife Service was moving to lift the refugium restrictions from the top of Mt. Graham.

III. The Desecration of a Shrine

And so the surrogate species approach had failed.

Radical interests that sought only to stifle development of an astrophysical site on Mt. Graham believed wholeheartedly they could do so by attaching their efforts to an "endangered species" that was listed solely to provide them with that tool.

Meanwhile, the University survived an avalanche of frivolous legal proceedings, dozens of ridiculous on-site protests with militant environmentalists wearing squirrel suits, chaining themselves to road-graders, blocking roads with fallen trees and vandalizing heavy equipment, and accusations of political corruption and coercion. Iconoclastic Dr. Robin Silver filed lawsuits against the U.S. Congress for acting illegally when passing the Arizona-Idaho Conservation Act of 1988, and against a public information officer at the University for his statements of fact to the media!

(Desperate tactics employed by the Dr. Silver breed of radical when faced with defeat of an ideal might be laughable if they weren't so vindictive.)

So what now? There must be another way.

Let's raise the issue of ancient religion!

The same opponents who rode the red squirrel issue to dismal failure helped to organize a Tucson-based group and named it the "Apache Survival Coalition." Suddenly it's revealed that the high peaks of Mt. Graham are sacred sites of Apache worship. The group, led by Apache activist Ola Cassadore Davis, filed suit against the Forest Service for allowing the desecration of their holy shrine.

Members of the Apache Survival Coalition include the same non-Native American environmental opponents active in the prior Sierra Club effort, and Coalition lawyers presented many of the same arguments made in the Sierra Club lawsuit. Again, the University (apparent target of the litigation) intervened as a co-defendant.

The San Carlos Apache Reservation boundary passes within 25 miles of Mt. Graham. However, San Carlos officials have shunned representation by, participation in, and specific claims made through the Apache Survival Coalition. In early 1993, representatives of the San Carlos Apache Tribe traveled to Europe to dispel unfavorable propaganda being pumped by telescope opponents to Vatican and Max Planck Institute officials. Later in the year, San Carlos Tribal Chairman Harrison Talgo and most members of the Tribal Council visited the observatory site and voiced support and enthusiasm for the project.

Some tribal members at San Carlos sincerely believe _some_ areas of the Pinaleno Mountains are sacred, but others do not. University officials have expressed their respect for genuine concerns raised by bona fide tribal members, and are working toward an accommodation with them—just as astronomers and the Tohono O'odham Tribe reconciled differences over the Kitt Peak Observatory near Tucson more than three decades earlier. Further, representatives of the University and San Carlos Apaches are working together on many concerns from agriculture, education and economic development to mineral exploration and development of a cultural museum.

The Apache Survival Coalition represents no Native American tribe; it is only a front—another "surrogate species," so to speak—contrived and fueled by the Sierra Club Legal Defense Fund in their ongoing struggle to choke down positive development.

A federal judge in Phoenix denied the Coalition lawsuit.

As expected, the Coalition appealed.

While awaiting a ruling on the appeal from the Ninth Circuit Court of Appeals, work was completed on the first two telescopes.

Throughout the process, Ola Cassadore Davis has kept the media supplied with a barrage of accusatory correspondences (some probably written or inspired by someone else). The diatribes contain unrealistically idyllic passages like " . . . on behalf of the cultural survival and religious freedom of all Native Americans and indigenous peoples worldwide . . . ," and ridiculously vague and uninformed verbiage like " . . . studies by 20 top U.S. institutions (who?) in the '80s . . . found Mt. Graham had serious visibility problems (gross untruth) . . . ," et cetera.

While the controversy rages, it becomes painfully obvious that the voices of protest and opposition all hail from outside the area which stands to be impacted most dramatically by development of a small observatory on a big mountain. The residents of rural Graham County, Arizona—who know and love the unique characteristics of this "sky island" more than anyone—are *not* the ones filing lawsuits and screaming foul.

Here, supporters see the benefits of a "clean" industry—no pollution of the air, soil or waterways. They appreciate the addition of new jobs, support services and tourism influx the observatory will add to the local economy. They know firsthand the appearance of the mountain has not been affected, nor will it be. Ecology management has only improved—and will continue to do so. They are excited about being chosen as the location from whence future astrophysical research will lead the world to a better understanding of the galaxies.

Their voices are not heard by the media, however, because they are not voices of protest. Supportive voices seldom make news. Sensationalism sells. An angry Apache woman decrying the rape of ancient Indian religion makes salable newsprint. It doesn't matter that she's inspired and supported by non-Indian preservationists. Wild-eyed eco-terrorists chaining their necks to cattle guards provide video footage for the evening news. No one asks who bought their plane tickets or gasoline to transport them from other parts of the country.

There is no news in the fact that Mt. Graham is _not_ being bulldozed to resemble a high flat mesa, or that wildlife populations are _increasing_ with concerted management practices.

The alliance between meddling uninformed outsiders and desperate ratings-driven journalists is epitomized by a story in the _Mesa Tribune_ by columnist Betty Webb. Rock star Eddie Vedder with the group Pearl Jam addressed an equally uninformed (and impressionable) young Mesa audience with graphic vulgarity and ignorance: "U of A, F--K YOU if you go ahead and develop Mount Graham!" Vedder then burned a UA sweatshirt on stage and performed a spasmodic dance around it. (Of course, he was paid handsomely for all of this).

Webb characterized Vedder as a glorified crusader, showering him with syrupy gushes of praise . . . and neither one of them has even been close to the telescope project on Mt. Graham. It is the classic calamity of ignorance perpetuating ignorance, and because Vedder _said_ it from the stage and Webb _wrote_ it in a newspaper, then "it" becomes gospel.

(If only it were so easy to spread the truth.)

IV. **A Part of Something Bigger**

The Pearl Jam concert was sponsored by the Apache Survival Coalition, who in turn is supported by the organized opponents of development on Mt. Graham. However, the bazaar Mt. Graham story is but an isolated subplot in a much broader drama.

First, it is not an oversimplification to say the impact of the observatory on Mt. Graham can be compared to the placing of a new pebble in the middle of a graveled road. And it is equally as compatible with its surroundings.

Additionally, the Sierra Club revealed the true nature of their opposition to the project in 1993. While applying the finishing touches to the first two telescopes, the University filed a request with the Fish and Wildlife Service to allow construction of the third scope at a different location—about a half-mile away where fewer trees would be disturbed and any potential impact on red squirrels would be decreased. Also, telescope images would be clearer.

Project opponents *objected!*

Abandoning all previous claims for red squirrels, old-growth trees and hallowed ground, vindictive antagonists responded this time in an obvious move to make life less simple for project officials. They objected and the FWS stalled. With no likelihood of a permit forthcoming, the University decided to stay at the original site on Emerald Peak and withdrew its request.

If the issue ever was concern for an endangered subspecies of squirrel, or for the preservation of old spruce and fir trees on the top of a mountain, then the relocation of the third telescope would have been welcomed with open arms.

However, that is *not* the case . . . nor seldom is it.

There is an attitude among preservationists today that *any* development is bad and must be stopped. This nation would never have become industrialized had the same mind-set existed early in the 20th century because nothing would have gotten built. There would be no dams for generating hydroelectric power, no powerlines to carry the voltage, no pipelines for transporting fuels, no mines for harvesting metals and minerals, no industrial parks or airports, no prisons for incarcerating convicts, no super highways, no factories or farms or sawmills, no subdivisions, theme parks, golf courses, and (for damn sure!) no observatories.

(We would all live naked in caves, eat dirt, and serve our gods—The Animals.)

There are *thousands* of stories across the U.S. where development has been thwarted because radical environmentalists, preservation extremists, regulation-obsessed bureaucrats, noetic earth worshipers, uncontrolled federal agencies, government-blessed independent agencies, jaded politicians—*somebody*—threw up insurmountable roadblocks.

(Try to imagine the ensuing furor today should someone propose a new interstate highway through the "critical habitat" of the endangered desert tortoise! Thank Providence there is already a ground route from Phoenix to Las Vegas and on to Los Angeles.)

So, how does the saga of Mt. Graham relate to the war on property rights or the erosion of the American Dream?

It all becomes one when you think of federally managed land as belonging to *all* the people of the land. It exists because it is not privately owned and, therefore, belongs to *all the people of the nation.* The federal government is an amalgam if its people. It is *not* a supreme being without a creator. It is not a sovereign entity. People from the various states created the federal government. *States* are sovereign, and *people* are sovereign, but the federal government is not.

The federal government works at the pleasure of the states and their citizens—or so it was intended. That is why the Constitution spells out a method for *abolishing* the federal government. A two-thirds majority vote of the *states* within the Union—votes cast by the *people*—can abolish the federal government, but the federal government has no method for abolishing the states or the people.

Washington powercrats have forgotten this. They feel they are invincible, and they are bothered that *all* is not under their control. A movement is on to abolish the rights of the people. *That* involves the owners of private land, the users of government-held lands, and developers of both. The assault is coming from many fronts (as illustrated in previous chapters and expanded upon in Part Four).

The cornerstone of democracy—our U.S. Constitution—is being hammered at with a growing ferocity; stroke by stroke, its integrity and ideals are being chipped away. None too soon, a resistance is mounting, but the fight will be fierce. Preserving the stellar notions of our founding fathers will come at a high price.

V. **An Afterword**

With the coming of spring, 1994, two telescopes were in use at the Mt. Graham International Observatory.

The Heinrich Hertz Submillimeter Telescope (known as the SMT) is the most accurate radio telescope ever built. Its radio wavelengths are the shortest that can pass relatively unimpeded through the earth's atmosphere. This sensitive instrument will become an important tool in exploring the process of star and planet formation both within our own Milky Way galaxy, and other galaxies throughout the universe. The $8,000,000 SMT is jointly operated by the University of Arizona and the Max Planck Institute for Radio Astronomy in Bonn, Germany. Modern astronomers believe the SMT will expand the boundaries of knowledge in virtually every facet of astronomical research.

The Vatican Advanced Technology Telescope (or VATT) is a $3,000,000 astronomical facility that will produce extremely sharp optical and infrared images. It is a joint effort of the Vatican Observatory near Castel Gandolfo, Italy, and the University of Arizona Steward Observatory. Vatican astronomers will study stars in the process of becoming main-sequence stars like the earth's sun, perhaps forming planets of their own, and will share the VATT with talented young scholars from developing nations as part of a program to aid young scientists from the world's less advanced countries.

(All this technology and promise for the future sits almost reclusively amid the towering conifers on a space amounting to less than 1/200,000th of the total land area of the mountain.)

April 5, 1994, was declared an "international day of action for Mt. Graham" by members of the militant environmental group Earth First! Protesters assembled in small groups at universities and Catholic churches in various cities across the country. An organizer wrote in an Earth

First! newsletter, " . . . we are now poised to win the war and get the scopes off Mt. Graham."

While their determination can only be admired, little can be said for their sense of perspicacity. The telescopes have congressional authorization, and they are on the mountain to stay. As construction proceeds on the Large Binocular Telescope (the most powerful land-based telescope in the world), many hundreds of on-site visitors are *seeing* the truth. Again, opposition to the project is not coming from those who live near it and will be most affected by it. No one from the surrounding communities participated in the April 5th demonstrations.

Some minor partners (the University of Michigan and the University of Pittsburgh) have withdrawn their financial support from what they view as a "culturally and environmentally sensitive" project.

On April 8, 1994, the Ninth U.S. Circuit Court of Appeals in San Francisco rejected a legal challenge to the observatory project by the Apache Survival Coalition. The Coalition claimed the "sacred" mountain was being defiled and sought relief under a federal law that protects historic and cultural sites. The lawsuit was thrown out on the basis that the Coalition filed their objections only after construction was well underway, and the San Carlos Apache tribe had ignored the observatory's planning process for six years.

And so, while the Mt. Graham ecosystem improves and red squirrel populations increase, informed supporters of the Mt. Graham International Observatory are forced to continue to fight a costly and senseless battle with vindictive detractors.

IV:

THE UNTOUCHABLE LAND

I. Crowned King of Old-Growth Forest

There's a movement afoot to expel *everyone* from federally controlled lands, no matter their reason for being there. Congressman Jim Kolbe, representing a district in southern Arizona, says the sentiment exists widely in Washington, although politicians and bureaucrats still will not openly admit it.

Varied are the reasons for this activity.

Some Eastern congressmen have seen pictures of isolated clear-cuts and been told all the mountains in the West are bare. Others hear words like "over-grazing" and conjure pictures of dust-bowl prairies and eroded hillsides. Most are targeted heavily by the affluent preservationist lobby, who knows politicians must raise campaign dollars to be reelected. All of them can somehow justify their conviction to "save" the West.

Not many of them listen to the voices of the people who *live* in the West—the "first environmentalists" who run the cattle and work the claims, harvest the timber, raise their families and pay their taxes, and manage the resources for renewal through the generations.

Most of them have never seen the West and haven't a clue as to its bone-and-fiber—its evolution and heritage, resources and culture, its people and space. They can't conceive of a land where it takes a hundred acres to graze a cow and calf, when five such pairs might roam fat on a single acre in Mississippi or Vermont. They don't know the pride of a rancher coaxing a trickle of water from the ground beneath his windmill, when lethargic rivers run deep and plentiful in Tennessee and Ohio. They have not seen the teams of foresters planting thousands of evergreen seedlings behind the logging crews.

Somehow the unrealistic vision of a "reinvented" West has been sold to an unfamiliar and gullible East. The sale, however, was not made singlehandedly; the pitch came from many sides, and still does. Environmental radicals decry any form of development as a rape of the landscape. Preservation extremists will sacrifice entire economies and municipalities for the protection of non-contributing insects and rodents and trash fish. Federal bureaucrats continue to hunger and strive for total control.

The West is so large and diverse that those who seek to claim it know it cannot be done with a single assault. So, a strategy has been developed to attack the various camps of resistance individually.

In one of those battles—the fight for western timber—the Clinton Administration promised a "balanced solution" to a crisis precipitated by the northern spotted owl listing. However, the Clinton environmental-yuppie mentality will not rule in favor of the 85,000 industry workers who have lost (and continue to lose) their jobs.

The Clinton plan calls for reducing the timber harvest of the federal forests in the Pacific Northwest to about one-fifth of the traditional level. Forests in the Cascade Mountains of Oregon and Washington are richer and fuller now, after decades of harvest and reforestation, than they've been at any time since before Lewis and Clark. Yet, a part of the Clinton plan for timber management suggests *importing lumber from other countries!*

There's also a provision for spending more than a billion dollars on regional programs for vocational training and community relief.

(These people don't need retraining or relief; they need their culture and economies back!)

Oregon Representative Bob Smith noted, "No amount of economic assistance, worker retraining or sympathy can change the fact that tens of thousands of family-wage jobs (are) lost."

The Clinton plan guarantees that lumber prices will continue to escalate, causing the price of homes to increase and sales to drop *nationwide*. Large numbers of western families and small communities will be sacrificed, as the result of the chokehold preservationists have upon a sympathetic administration.

The "New West" philosophy is a Utopian ideal gone mad. Preservationists are pulling the strings. The

Administration is a dangling puppet lacking backbone enough to act without consulting the Sierra Club first. Sierra Legal Defense Fund lawyer Todd True said in late 1993, "It is premature to talk about (releasing) any particular amount" of timber.

Interior Department Chief of Staff Tom Collier revealed appeasingly that the preservationists agreed to "work with the Administration" to devise a list of timber sales they would not oppose should the Administration "ask for permission" to resume logging.

(Who do *you* think is calling the shots?)

Still determined to control every tree in the forest (the issue is *not* spotted owls), the above concession on the part of the Sierra Club was accompanied by a "condition"—that their generosity be rewarded by a guarantee from the Administration that Congress will not be allowed to modify their final forest plan.

U.S. District Court Judge William Dwyer issued the original injunction against logging in spotted owl forests in 1991. Since then, the timber industry has all but died in the Pacific Northwest. The impact on economies, communities and families was never a factor—only the blind determination of radical eco-preservationists who stand to lose nothing, and find ready support among pontifical judges and dogmatic politicians.

In the Cascade Mountains 30 miles east of Sweet Home, Oregon, a brutal windstorm has flattened dozens of square miles of old-growth forest. Millions of board feet of timber lay rotting, thousands of old Douglas firs crisscrossed like matchsticks, twisted and broken. Each year the impending threat of catastrophic fire grows. The inflexible nature of preservationist logic (and Judge Dwyer's injunction) will not allow cleanup and reforestation of the mountain, for such activity might disturb a spotted owl.

While the entire controversy demonstrates environmental lunacy, it also reflects a glaring irony. Would clearing the broken windfalls create more disturbance than the wind blowing them down? At one time, the board footage in those trees was salvageable. Now, they invite harmful insects, flirt with fire hazard, and provide no habitat for owls—only danger.

(Another example of surrogate species being used to achieve the real end. The owl is not the issue; *public* use of the land is.)

Another irony swells in the lives of northwestern timber workers in communities throughout Oregon and Washington. While the numbers facing loss of livelihood increase with each move of the eco-preservationists and their Administration cohorts, unemployed and displaced workers meet in coffee shops to discuss the future. They also remember the past.

They recall a time when the Forest Service was a regulator and still a partner in their industry. They worked together for wise management of the forest and perpetuation of an industry and culture. They provided the stock from which homes were built around the world. And there was a pride in their partnership.

Today, there is suspicion, distance and anger.

The timbermen know that by congressional mandate the Forest Service, upon its creation, was obligated to provide "community stability" in the locales of its management operation. A system for coordinating efforts between the agency and local governments was established.

Today, that process has been forsaken.

"Community stability" is defined as a combination of custom, culture and economic preservation. The Forest Service itself outlines the "History and Objects of Forest Reserves": " . . . *for the purposes of preserving a perpetual supply of timber for home industries, preventing destruction of the forest cover which regulates the flow of streams, and protecting local residents from unfair competition in the use of the range . . . that the welfare of every community is dependent upon a cheap and plentiful supply of timber . . . "*

Today, just as with constitutionally guaranteed private property rights and the well-meant passage of endangered species protection, the intent of this governmental brainchild has been lost and forgotten by activists and bureaucrats who cannot reason beyond their own self-serving agendas.

The ironies have not escaped the people in timber-dependent communities. They ponder but don't understand how the same government that leaps to the aid of flood-swept farms in the Midwest or riot-torn inner cities can take deliberate action (or nonaction) to wipe out entire communities and economies in other regions. Neither do they comprehend the contradictions within an administration that promises to create jobs while strangling entire industries.

The Administration is allowing (even facilitating) the loss of hundreds of millions of dollars in federal timber receipts and taxes generated through the lumber industry. Lumber prices will continue to soar, and first-time home buyers will be generated only from an elite group of affluent young people.

(Another chunk is chiseled from the American Dream.)

None of this is about protecting spotted owls. It is not about saving old-growth forests. It is about removing the public from unappropriated lands. It is about centralized control of an entire country by an enormous enviro-bureaucracy.

The American public needs to know they are being played by the preservationist movement like so many pieces on a gigantic chessboard. They are the victims of an unending tidal wave of misinformation, propaganda and outright lies told so often they take on "lives" of their own. The media become unwitting (or intentional) partners in the ploy because, for the most part, journalists don't know the difference between environmental truth and fiction. The sensational verbiage of eco-radicals makes far more salable newsprint than sensible people telling plain truths.

The whole timber industry debacle was precipitated by an environmental claim that a dwindling population of northern spotted owls would become extinct if logging continued in old-growth forests. The assertion was uttered and repeated until it became "fact" to naive nature-lovers across the country.

Puzzling it is, then, that researchers Greg Miller, employed by the Bureau of Land Management Eugene District, and Dennis Rock, of the National Council on Air and Stream Improvement, have found 14 pairs of NSOs living in lower-elevation, second-growth timberlands east of Springfield, Oregon. The owls seem very comfortable and well-adapted to young forest areas that have been clear-cut or burned, sprayed with herbicides and replanted, all in the last six to eight decades.

Another "*un*truism" spouted liberally by preservationists draws a bleak picture of ravaged mountaintops in the Pacific Northwest jutting obscenely amidst the remaining ten percent of old-growth forests that must now be saved from the rape of loggers' chainsaws and bulldozers. Tennessee Senator Al Gore—before becoming Vice President of the United States—either believed the scenario as told to him, or chose to perpetuate a lie, when he repeated the claim in his book *Earth in Balance*.

A conflicting opinion (and a more honest one) comes from Roger Sedjo, a forestry expert working for the nonpartisan group Resources for the Future. Sedjo claims that forestry practices and forest conditions hit their lowest ebb about 1920. Sedjo writes: "Sometime around 1940, forest growth nationally came into balance with harvests, and since that time, growth has exceeded harvest." He cites as an example the state of Vermont, which was 35 percent forested 100 years ago, and boasts more than twice that amount today.

More specifically related to timber management in the Pacific Northwest, Oregon and Washington today have more than 6,500 square miles of old-growth forests in permanent reserve. These areas will *never* be logged, and the timber industry is not asking that any of this be changed. If these old-growth timberlands were strung out together in a continuous two-mile-wide strip across the country, they would reach from Portland, Oregon, to Portland, Maine, and right on out into the ocean on both sides of this continent.

Radical environmental doomsayers espouse the urgency of saving a unique owl species virtually on the brink of extinction, no matter the cost. However, various reports and population surveys quickly substantiate the existence of more than 3,000 nesting pairs of NSOs, while California condors and western snowy plovers are known to number only in the tens.

" . . . a unique owl species?"

Even the Sierra Club Legal Defense Fund, who has represented lawsuits of every imaginable description on behalf of the NSO, has admitted the owl was listed as a surrogate to protect the ancient forests of the Northwest. It is no longer strongly arguable that NSOs fare better in old-growth than in second- or third-growth forests. There has not been a genetic difference shown between the NSO and other species of spotted owls known to inhabit most of the western U.S.

(Similarly, the California spotted owl and the Mexican spotted owl have been listed as surrogates to halt logging in California, Colorado, Arizona and New Mexico. These "species," too, were listed without a preponderance of data to support their impending extinction.)

Scientists have also found themselves trying to explain the crossbreeding of at least two northern spotted owls with two common barred owls in the northern Cascade Range in Washington. Eric Forsman, a Forest Service biologist, said, "I don't know where it's going to lead us." The confirmed incidents do raise a couple of questions rather quickly. One, are we faced now with the "birth" of a _new_ "endangered species"? And, frankly, is the northern spotted owl unique at all?

" . . . no matter the cost" is an _under_-understatement!

In 1990 alone, the federal government spent $9,600,000 guarding the northern spotted owl. Further, it is estimated that _each nesting pair_ of NSOs will end up costing American taxpayers about $916,000. Another calculation comes from Gardner Brown, an economics and environmental studies professor at the University of Washington, and Claire Montgomery, an assistant professor of forestry at the University of Montana. The pair of scholars completed a study in 1993 explicating a price tag of $21,000,000,000 (that's _billion_) for an 82 percent chance at survival for the NSOs. When the survival rating is raised to 95 percent, the price goes up to $46,000,000,000.

(Wake up, folks! Does anyone truly believe the Sierra Club, the Audubon Society, the Oregon Natural Resource Council, or any other nest of eco-radicals, will stand good for this expense? No, the American _public_ will foot the bill.)

Urban and eastern dwellers who think the northern-spotted-owl-versus-timber-industry war is "somebody else's problem" should brace for an abrupt collision with reality. The average American home uses about 15,000 board feet of dimensional lumber and 8,000 square feet of plywood.

Timber industry analyst Paul Ehinger of Eugene, Oregon, says, "Prices are going through the roof (and) . . . there's not the wood to put through the mills." From 1991 to 1993, the increase in construction costs to an average home attributed solely to the price of lumber was $5,000.

As long as the preservation extremists and bureaucrats choke down the American timber industry, consumers can only expect to see this trend continue. Importing lumber from across the seas will not make prices go down. One sawmill in Klamath Falls, Oregon, has brought in logs from Utah on railcars, but that too is costly and will only help to preserve some local jobs for awhile; it will not help to stabilize or reduce the cost of new homes.

The Clinton Administration, as a part of the "plan" that will supposedly fix all the problems of the timber industry, suggests pumping millions of dollars into retraining displaced workers, and importing lumber from overseas. Forests in Russia, Malaysia, Indonesia, Japan, Canada and Brazil are being targeted for massive logging operations as a result of the industry shutdown in the Pacific Northwest. Most countries outside the U.S. have little or no forest management or reclamation programs.

(Is a tree in the Northwest more important than a tree in the Far East? Are foreign ecosystems more expendable than our own?)

Despite the scare tactics and quixotic rhetoric commonly used by clever eco-fanatics, logging is good for the ecosystem. A regulated timber industry equates to eco-management. Forests are renewable. America possesses vast timberlands that are capable of renewing themselves to eternity for wildlife and water conservation, recreation and tourism—and timber.

(Remember, the national forest system was created more than a century ago to provide a continuous supply of lumber to meet the country's growing needs *forever*.)

If man does not harvest and reforest, then nature will burn and reseed. The most glaring example in recent times was the burning of Yellowstone National Park in the late 1980s after decades of hands-off management allowed the natural canopy to become a tinderbox. Northwest reforesting operations have averaged planting six to ten trees for each one harvested. In 1989 alone, 130,000,000 trees were planted in Oregon forests. Strict environmental laws in the Pacific Northwest (supported by timbermen) mandate that logged areas must be *successfully* reforested within five years of harvest . . . and harvesting operations are forbidden from taking more board footage than will grow in a given year.

Unmanaged forests fall victim to numerous maladies. Bark beetles thrive where timberlands are left untended. Natural decay, root disease, dwarf mistletoe and other diseases take their toll. Without management, they become rampant. Sound environmental and economic practices once allowed "salvage" operations to clean the forest of affected and contagious members while they were still salable.

Logging is good for the "greenhouse effect" (if, in fact, there is such a thing). Scientists have determined that a growing forest absorbs about 6,000 pounds of carbon dioxide while producing some 4,000 pounds of oxygen. Conversely, an old-growth forest releases carbon dioxide and uses oxygen while decomposing. A study completed at the University of Maryland suggests that extensive logging (followed by reforestation) may have a *cooling* effect on the earth's atmosphere.

(The environmentalist who hypothesizes global warming while denouncing the timber industry is a hypocrite.)

Again, the movement afoot has nothing to do with saving owls or trees. It has everything to do with taking control of all the lands in a nation and the resources upon them. It has most of all to do with a government run by radical preservationists who know they'll never have total control as long as the masses believe in their forefathers' concept of "inalienable" rights.

II. **Thar's Politics in Them Thar Hills**

There's a movement afoot to expel everyone from government-managed lands, no matter their reason for being there.

Cy Jamison, a former director of the Bureau of Land Management during the Bush Administration, says the Clinton camp has "declared a war on the West." He says range reform proposals are running askew of laws requiring multiple use of federally managed western lands. Jamison points up the strategy being used by Interior Secretary Babbitt and others is to leave western people out of the process, and simply impose new restrictive regulations administratively.

In the 20-year period preceding the Civil War, nearly 400,000 Americans migrated west with visions of hope, promise and prosperity. Laws enacted by the government encouraged the opening and settling of the West. Farmers homesteaded land and ranchers claimed enormous ranges. The famed Oklahoma Land Grab of 1889 was merely an effort by the government to get more people onto more available land in the West.

Somewhere in the midst of all this it became apparent that a lot of western migration was inspired by the lure of vast riches. The discovery of gold and silver at many locations throughout the West brought fortune-seekers in droves.

Congress enacted a law in 1872 that would effectively regulate the mining industry for the next 120 years. The law set up a standard of rights and behavior with respect to the use of unappropriated lands for mining and exploration, for claiming minerals beneath the surface by large and small operations, and by lone prospectors. It set the guidelines for the evolution of a new western culture and tradition.

With the arrival of Bruce Babbitt on the scene as Interior Secretary in 1993, another sector of the American West found itself facing annihilation. With liberal leftist allies like Representatives Nick Joe Rahall of West Virginia and George Miller of California teaming with radical anti-mining activist Phil Hocker, Babbitt's onslaught of American rights and customs became a foregone conclusion. New legislation was drafted that would gut the Mining Law of 1872, and impose penalties and restrictions enough to destroy the mining industry in the U.S.

There's a naive mentality displayed by some of the lawmakers who will decide the fate of thousands of western families and their livelihoods. Representative Carolyn Maloney from Manhattan granted a meeting in her office to a group of mining supporters during which an aide to the congresswoman remarked, "I know mining is important to you out West, but we don't use much metal in New York."

(Excuse me . . ? Is there *life* in there? New York is *made* of metal and wood and stone—*all* of which were harvested from the earth!)

These people—eastern bureaucrats and politicians who have never seen, cannot comprehend and do not appreciate the West—are going to contribute to future decisions that will set the stage for western livelihood. In reality, the economic structure of the United States will not survive the demise of mining activity on western lands—no matter the idyllic eastern vision of a "New West."

Nevada alone, where mining constitutes 12 percent of the state's total gross product, generated 6,000,000 ounces of gold in 1990. That's 62 percent of all the gold produced in the U.S. that year, and 11 percent of the world's production.

(Dentists alone used 292,000 ounces of gold during the same time period.)

Mining companies invested $5,000,000,000 in Nevada in the five years preceding 1991, and the same period saw employment in the state's mining industry climb from 6,000 jobs to 16,000 jobs. State and local taxes paid by the mining industry increased from $21,000,000 in 1986 to $90,000,000 in 1991.

Arizona, the number one producer of hardrock minerals in the nation, enjoys a $7,300,000,000 economic benefit with 19,000 workers employed in the mining industry. Dave Ridinger, Executive Director of the Arizona Mining Association, says the reform provisions in the new mining legislation of 1993 will stop new mining development dead in its tracks. Many small operations on government-run lands will be forced by high punitive royalties to shut down. Larger existing operations on private property will continue to produce only as long as ore supplies last, or until government regulation prices them out of business.

As many as 44,000 jobs stand to disappear.

Eastern manufacturing facilities processing materials mined in the West will be affected. Congressman Jim Kolbe of Arizona says, "The ripple effect of destroying an industry that contributes minerals for millions of American products would be enormous." Kolbe's Arizona colleague Congressman Jon Kyl cites a study showing a combined loss of output and earnings over a ten-year period beginning in 1993 will result in a *net loss* at the U.S. Treasury Department of about $422,000,000.

None of this means a thing to the eco-visionaries who seek to possess and control the West. Kyl says the Mineral Exploration and Development Act of 1993 is less about correcting abuses of the Mining Law of 1872 than it is about trying to shut down virtually all mining operations on federally managed lands, no matter how well-run those operations are.

It's interesting to note that all the environmental panic and political urgency is over a relatively small amount of land area. To put it in perspective, there are 2,270,000,000 total land acres in the U.S. About 662,000,000 of those acres are unappropriated lands. Less than 6,000,000 acres are utilized for mining purposes.

Again, this is only about removing the public from government-controlled lands.

Thousands of small miners are being driven from western lands by regulations imposed through the Bureau of Land Management. An amendment to the Department of the Interior Appropriations Act of 1993 erased a provision in the 1872 Mining Law which allowed small miners to perform the equivalent of $100 in assessment work on private mining claims annually. Instead (on very short, poorly publicized notice), the holders of small claims, many of them passed down through generations of western prospecting families, were forced to pay a $100-per-claim rental fee for 1993, plus another $100-per-claim advance rental fee for 1994.

While Mineral Policy Center bullhorn Phil Hocker called the rental fee a "minor adjustment," 465,000 valid claims were forced out of existence—many of them because families could not afford the rental fees, and others because they didn't know in time. In a single sweep, the DOI had managed to reduce the number of claimholders on unappropriated lands by a whopping 61 percent.

It will get worse.

The Mining Exploration and Development Act contains disastrous language (not unintentionally so). The law imposes a punitive eight percent gross royalty which makes most operations unprofitable. It requires unreasonable reclamation requirements (such as the possible refilling of a half-mile-deep open pit at Morenci, Arizona, at a cost of $2,000,000,000). And it mandates a land-planning process for _all_ government-held lands to determine the suitability for mining with criteria so broad that nearly any area can be closed to mining at the whim of a federal land manager.

There will never be a new mine developed within the U.S.

Congressman Kolbe says the law represents "the wholesale dismantling of the hardrock mining industry."

Dave Ridinger says, "Mining is migrating south of the border."

Such is the case, as well, with the domestic oil industry. While the industry has responded to cries of environmental foul by cleaning up wellsites, rerouting pipelines, improving refining technology and promoting a minimal disturbance approach to exploration and production, the government has imposed layer upon layer of new rules and regulations.

Large oil companies are closing up shop throughout the U.S. Smaller operations are abandoning domestic projects. More than a dozen major corporations—from Exxon, Chevron and Shell to Amoco, Mobil and True Oil—

blame escalating costs of environmental compliance as a pivotal factor in their diminishing profits.

As with most obsessions, environmental lunacy creates the potential for disastrous consequences. Congress, inspired by eco-protectionists' intense lobbying efforts, move to ensure environmental safeguards at all costs. They force increased traffic on the high seas. Based on projected consumption of petroleum products in the U.S., within a few years as many as 36 supertankers carrying 500,000 barrels of crude oil each will dock daily at domestic ports. The odds for an oil spill resulting from a tanker accident are 50 times greater than a platform spill—*at 1993 traffic levels*—and the volume of oil is *1,500 times greater!*

Terry Donze, President of the Denver Geophysical Society, says it's time for the environmental community to wake up to the consequences of their actions. Private industry has spent more than $1,400,000,000,000 (that's 1.4 *trillion*) on environmental programs and mandates. The demand has only just begun.

Donze writes, "With that cost comes a loss of personal and economic freedom, loss of private sector investment that spurs technological growth, destabilization of government through voluntary and involuntary noncompliance of a maze of unscientific and often conflicting regulations, increased dependency on unstable countries for our raw materials, and its associated loss of security and power in the world."

A couple of appropriate bumper sticker slogans come readily to mind at this juncture. The first one promotes a simple truism: *If it can't be grown, then it must be mined.*

Living in a world where natural resources are off-limits is not an intelligent concept. Food, clothing, homes, automobiles, and everything else humans (including preservationists) take for granted in the course of daily living, come from the earth. Fuel for transportation, power generation for heating homes and offices, come from the earth. Glass and high-technology fiber-optics are made of sand from the earth. Health foods and vitamin supplements originate from the earth. Rubber, copper, paper, salt, penicillin, propane, cotton are products of the earth.

If it can't be grown, then it must be mined, with one exception—plastics. Plastic is a synthetic substance being used in innovative ways to replace glass and steel and paper and other materials. Ironically, as it becomes more and more popular and adapted to new uses, it also has become the worse source of pollution in the world because it never deteriorates!

The other bumper sticker speaks for itself: *I love my country, but I fear my government.*

III. **Home, Home off the Range**

There's a movement afoot to expel everyone from western rangelands, no matter their reason for being there.

The worst day in history for private property owners and traditional federal lands users came when President Clinton appointed former Arizona Governor Bruce Babbitt to the office of Interior Chief. The Secretary has since demonstrated his unwavering allegiance to preservationist attitudes and the Endangered Species Act, and he has vowed to change the way lands are used on his way to creating a "New West."

Babbitt vowed, upon taking charge of the DOI, that 1993 would be "the year for public land reform." Repeatedly, on the issues of mining and ranching, the Secretary threatened to implement his own reforms without the approval of Congress. He made a poor display of attempting to placate the western public by conducting a whirlwind series of orchestrated "hearings," claiming the media he was "listening to the people."

Meanwhile, his real agenda was snaking through the Interior Department like a hungry python. Babbitt's penchant for slight-of-hand maneuvers became glaringly apparent in midsummer of 1993, even before his official announcement on "rangeland reform" was met with howls of disapproval from Democrats and Republicans alike.

The nature of the beast confronting all unappropriated western lands users reared its ugly head as an internal memo leaked from the Interior Department in late June of 1993. Written by staffers Kevin Sweeney and Lucia Wyman, the memo was sent to Babbitt and two of his lieutenants, Jim Baca and Tom Collier, outlining an underhanded approach to furthering their cause:

RE: Grazing Issues — One Disagreement, One Suggestion

1. Let's Not Issue Draft Regs with a Range of Possible Fees

A shift in the Administration's approach to mining and grazing revenues was the most visible sign of backsliding on the budget. Part of our role this summer is to help them get back on track—give them a clear victory in this area . . .

We realize you want to use price increases as a straw man to draw attention from management issues. But there are other ways this might be done . . .

We could . . . begin to talk about a range of possible fees during the month of July. We can do this through leaks, press releases, op-eds, whatever . . .

2. We need to Sell These Regs —in Advance

We've not yet done enough to sell the public and media on what will be coming out of the regs. We should work to justify what is in the regs before they actually come out.

There are two major changes which will come out in the regs, and we should construct a few events that help us justify those changes . . .

I. General Approach

Project Goal:

The following are the goals for this communications strategy . . .

> *Introduce the new regulations into a Western environment that is somewhat receptive, and*

> *manage the first public comments so the regs are perceived to be fair and in the long-tern interest of the region.*

Ultimate Story Lead:

We'd like stories and editorials to focus on the following points:

> *The new regulations show real balance . . .*
> *They recognize that many things are best done on the local level . . .*
> *The fee increases are not so bad . . .*

II. Steps Prior to Release of Regulations

Specific Goals:

Prior to the release, we should consider steps to adjust expectations in the following areas:

> *Riparian Zones. Our own statistics can be used to show the range is in better shape than at any point in this century.*
> *With that in mind, we must make deliberate and public attempts to prove how bad the conditions are in many riparian zones . . .*

The conspiratorial dissertation continues. From the beginning, Babbitt's vision of "range reform" has been a concerted effort to deceive the American public, using the gullible and easily misled media to facilitate the plan.

The plan would increase grazing fees by 130 percent, costing many small family-style ranching operations their entire livelihoods. However, the fee increase was only the tip of the iceberg. The federal government would take control of ranchers' vested water rights and rangeland improvements done at ranchers' expense. Grazing advisory boards would be replaced by *resource* advisory *councils* impregnated with eco-preservationists. All ranchers (on private land and otherwise) would be viewed and treated equally, regardless of geographic and other mitigating factors, and grazing permits would become more easily revoked and more difficult to retrieve.

Some astute westerners quickly saw through the haze and began to talk very loudly about the underlying negative implications in the reform plan. Washington lawmakers began dividing into camps with some powerful and respected Democrats leading the opposition to Administration bulldozing alongside Republican stalwarts.

The autumn months of 1993 saw a flurry of activity on Capitol Hill with the Senate placing a one-year freeze on any plan to raise grazing fees. The House overturned the moratorium and passed a compromise version of Babbitt's plan that would have raised grazing fees by 85 percent. Of that action, Arizona Congressman Jim Kolbe said, "This deal was brokered . . . in the dead of night behind closed doors with no input from lawmakers whose states will be drastically affected . . . "

Some western senators, including Pete Domenici of New Mexico, organized a filibuster to block the legislation. Senator John McCain of Arizona said, "We have all seen how federal policies affecting the timber industry on public lands can wreak havoc on small towns . . . The cattle industry is of critical importance to the well-being of many rural communities in Arizona. It has a $302,000,000 annual impact on Arizona's economy."

Senators Ben Nighthorse Campbell and Hank Brown of Colorado, Malcolm Wallop and Alan Simpson of Wyoming, Larry Craig and Dirk Kempthorne of Idaho, Robert Bennett and Orrin Hatch of Utah, Conrad Burns of Montana and others (a telling mix of Democrats and

Republicans), contributed eloquently and courageously to the success of the filibuster.

Lawmakers were forced to pare reform authorization language from the Interior Department's 1994 funding bill so the DOI would have money to continue operations.

(Yes, the Administration thought they had concealed the range reform provisions cleverly enough within an appropriations bill that a slight compromise on grazing fees alone would allow the Clinton-Babbitt conspiracy to become law.)

The curtain closed on this Capitol Hill scene in November of 1993. It was not the final act of the play, however. Secretary Babbitt, angered by what he called "reform that never seems to happen", declared he would implement his proposals through the administrative rule-making process in 1994, thereby bypassing any need for congressional approval.

Traditional users of federally controlled lands in the West can only hope Congress has the strength and dedication to override Babbitt's plan. Lawmakers have that *right*, but do they have the clout? Visionaries of the "New West" are betting they don't because a lot of high-paid, high-powered eco-lobbyists apply themselves to the Capitol Hill mainstream daily. Senators and congressmen from anywhere but the West—who have not the time nor the desire to learn about the West—prefer to rely on misinformation peddled by special interests who can help them get reelected.

The critical nature of western lands reform is epitomized in a small county in western New Mexico—Senator Domenici's home state. The 2,700 residents of Catron County lived traditionally by the labor and product generated solely from two industries—timber and cattle. The timber industry died after 1990, as the direct result of Mexican spotted owl protection and forest management practices. Continued enforcement of the Endangered Species Act, as well as the push to further restrict federal land use, threatens the county's single remaining means of livelihood.

There are no alternatives for Catron County.

Western New Mexico University conducted a series of detailed studies to define or identify other possible industries for the area. Researchers found that tourism and recreation showed the greatest promise of economic salvation. However, in a ten-year period, tourism/recreation would only generate about $4,800,000 per year, while livestock production in 1993 produced $20,000,000. That equates to slashing a workman's salary from $2,000 a month to $480.

(The constitutional protection of customs and cultures should apply here somewhere.)

There are 165 family-owned ranches in Catron County.

In 1990, the Southwest Center for Resource Analysis at Western New Mexico University compiled a socioeconomic study of the impacts of grazing fee increases on five New Mexico ranching counties. Catron County used the information to construct its own projection of socioeconomic impact on all the citizens of the county.

With various proposals being brandished around Washington at the time, Catron County officials arbitrarily settled on a 40-percent grazing fee hike to use as a denominator. The analysis showed that implementation of a 40-percent fee increase would reduce the number of working ranches in the county to 99. The number of cattle in the county would decrease from 42,000 to 26,400. Cattle industry wages would fall from $943,500 to $566,100. Cattle industry jobs would plummet from 495 to 198, and ranch population would dip from 878 to 510. Cash receipts from cattle would crash from $20,700,000 in 1989 to $12,400,000 after the increase, and Catron County's total population would plunge to 1,100 people by the year 2000.

(Remember, this is all based on 40 percent. Babbitt wanted 130 percent, and the 1993 compromise called for 85 percent.)

With Babbitt's reforms in place, Catron County will die. Residents will be forced to abandon their homes to look for means of livelihood elsewhere. Schools will close. Houses will sit empty and deteriorate—made worthless by the absence of a supporting industry or healthy economy. A 400-year-old custom of livestock ranching in the hills of western New Mexico will succumb to bureaucratic greed and eco-madness. A once thriving culture will become a ghostly memory of the past.

The bureaucrats and preservationists don't care. To them, this is not about schools or houses, jobs or revenues, customs or cultures. It is about possessing and controlling unappropriated lands, and removing legitimate users from them—at all costs. Already in early 1994, Secretary Babbitt was conducting a series of *new* meetings in the West—purporting to include ranchers and politicians, environmentalists and recreationists in a plan for increased "local control" of rangeland policy—but interested parties found the meetings closed to anyone not personally invited.

There are many examples of statistics and circumstances that support cattle grazing as a healthy management practice.

A study conducted by the University of Oklahoma in 1950 showed that total living matter is greater in grazed pastures than in ungrazed pastures, and less organic content exists in ungrazed prairie soil than in the same soil when grazing is practiced.

In his revealing video *Wetlands Management in Today's Environment,* Nevada rancher Cliff Gardner shows the devastating effects of the no-people policy on the Malheur Wildlife Refuge. A 181,000-acre area 40 miles long and 37 miles wide once allowed 52 permit-holding ranchers to run cattle, to raise grain and cut hay. During that time, in the 1950s, the Malheur Refuge boasted a larger nesting population of greater sandhill cranes than any other refuge in the country. Tens of thousands of waterfowl and other marsh-related species inhabited the acreage.

By the early 1970s, dozens of permittees were being removed from the project. Wildlife began migrating to adjacent private farmland where the food supply was still intact. During the 1973-74 season, only two greater sandhill crane chicks were raised on the refuge itself.

Nevada, Utah and Colorado comprise the single area in the world where the Ute ladies tresses orchid is found. Concern for the rare flower caused a stir in Colorado where the Hogan Brothers Ranches raised hay and grazed cows. The Hogans were removed from the land in 1984 so the orchids could thrive undisturbed. Within a year, the plants had nearly disappeared. The Hogans returned and resumed cattle and haying operations. By 1991, thousands of Ute ladies tresses had responded again to the benefits of traditional ranching practices.

In 1991, the Bureau of Land Management reported that in the preceding 30 years elk populations had expanded by 800 percent. Bighorn sheep numbers were up by 435 percent, antelope by 112 percent, deer 33 percent, and moose populations had increased by a full 500 percent—all in areas where livestock generally share the range.

A BLM plan implemented for livestock control within a National Conservation Area near Safford, Arizona, focused on managed seasonal use of the Gila River and Bonita Creek. The plan utilized grazing systems, exclosures and riparian pastures. Water sources were developed on the "uplands" to minimize livestock dependency on water in the canyon bottom riparian areas. Resulting range improvements outside the NCA boundary include fences, pipelines, stock ponds, corrals, troughs, roads and line shacks. Improvements *within* the riparian areas are pumping stations to provide water to the uplands, water gaps, cattle guards and fences to control livestock, roads for access to and within the allotments, corrals and line shacks.

Six grazing allotments within the NCA have been responsible for "moderate positive impact" on riparian areas along the Gila River and Bonita Creek between major flood events (approximately ten years from 1983 to 1993). Bonita Creek was so improved that the BLM Safford District was presented a national award for excellence in riparian management (with cows included) by the American Fisheries Society.

Washington powercrats are not impressed, and the objectives of preservation radicals remain unchanged. This is not about awards for a job well done. It's has nothing to do with abused or improved rangeland, with increased wildlife population, with the absence of sandhill cranes or the presence of rare orchids.

It has only to do with the removal of people from the land—any way possible. Just as spotted owls and red squirrels have become "surrogates" in environmental battles against logging and telescopes, so are other species of plants and animals used to justify the end of traditional ranching practices in the West. When it's shown that deer and elk cohabit and flourish with cattle, the enviro-strategists will choose a more elusive ally. Arizona Game and Fish officials have decided cattle must be kept away from creeks in the White Mountains in order to protect the "threatened" Apache trout.

Ranching, logging and mining are embedded American cultures. Raw-muscled pioneers pursuing these endeavors fought blizzards and Indians, raging rivers and drought, rattlesnakes and sickness, to open the West to a burgeoning eastern civilization. They learned to feed cattle amidst the chaparral and sagebrush, and coax precious water from beneath a parched land. They devised ingenious methods of harvesting timber from treacherous mountains with handsaws, axes, oxen and flumes. They ferreted out metals and minerals from the bowels of a hostile earth, and developed methods of smelting, processing and refining their ores.

They provided the raw material for expanding a nation. They supplied the means for perpetuating and improving a civilization. They lived the American Dream and made it work for millions more. The United States Government encouraged them in their pursuits 200 years ago, but the attitude in Washington is different today. The Constitution of the United States promised them protection for their cultures and customs. Secretary of the Interior Bruce Babbitt and others with a common mind-set have forgotten that it still does.

IV. The United States of America National Park

They want it all—and they'll take it if they can.

At the end of 1993, the United States Government controlled about 40 percent of the total land area in the country. Another 17 to 20 percent was in the hands of other levels of government, most notably the individual states and their municipalities.

Dixy Lee Ray, the late former Governor of Washington and staunch defender of property rights, named the National Park Service as the federal agency most active in transferring land from private ownership to government control. She said an ultimate goal of the NPS is to take all forests out of private hands.

Thousands of private landowners across the country have experienced the brunt of NPS greed.

Nellie Jenkins Woodward of Syria, Virginia, recalls the dark day in 1937 when the family home was lost to the NPS. Her mother was five months pregnant when two sheriffs carried her out. Her father, tears on his face, pleaded not to be handcuffed. Personal family belongings were thrown onto a horse-drawn wagon before federal agents broke windows and pushed down a chimney to discourage anyone from returning. Nellie, 16 at the time, saw her mother and the family's belongings dumped on the side of the road outside a place they called "The Poorhouse."

The Shenandoah National Park is billed as "Virginia's Mountain Playground," but a bitterness exists in the minds and hearts of former property owners and their descending families in the area. Even in the 1920s and '30s, deception and coercion and outright strong-arming were some tactics used by government officials to establish and acquire the Shenandoah.

Landowners within the 196,000 acres proposed for national park designation were frightened and outraged by the prospect of losing their properties. Having no organized voice, their cries of opposition went virtually unheard as affluent newsmakers joined the push for congressional designation. John D. Rockefeller, the Thomas A. Edison Estate, Edsel Ford, and Ball Brothers of Indiana all became major financial contributors to the acquisition of land to form the park in Virginia.

W.E. Carson, Chairman of the State Commission on Conservation and Development for Virginia, joined Interior Secretary Hubert Work in support of the project. George Freeman Pollock entertained influential guests at his Skyland Lodge, located within the proposed park area, extending the premise that Shenandoah National Park would be a playground and retreat for haggard factory workers and urban residents of the East.

Pollock intimated to Congress that no more than 1,500 people (landowners and families) would be affected by the formation of Shenandoah Park. In reality, there were 15,000!

Carson fought for and won the right to exercise blanket condemnations of private property. The landholders who refused to leave were physically removed or arrested by federal marshals, as their homes and barns were torched behind them. In the years to follow, the mountain families found they were barred from returning to the land, even to maintain the cemeteries where their deceased ancestors were buried.

In 1991, the NPS was working on a plan to enlarge Shenandoah National Park by an additional 327,000 acres. At least eight individual county governments affected by the proposed expansion rose up in adamant opposition. The Board of Supervisors in Madison County, Virginia, vowed to allow no "further acquisitions to this already mismanaged monster-playground."

Also in Virginia, the Manassas Battlefield Park was established in 1940. In 1990, U.S. taxpayers unknowingly paid $130,000,000 for 542 acres to be added to the park. No significant fighting ever occurred on the site. Neither were there graves nor other historic evidence on the property. Without success, local county supervisors opposed the NPS's acquisition of the land, and the loss of $23,000,000 in local tax revenues.

America's first national river was designated in Arkansas in 1972—the Buffalo National River. As virtuous and regal as the concept and implementation of such a project may sound, the grassroots reality of the matter again involved condemnation and confiscation of thousands of acres of private land and the displacement of hundreds of families.

The Buffalo National River contains more than 95,000 acres along 130 miles of the Buffalo River flowing through four counties. About 70 percent of the designated National River area is closed to the public—almost 40 percent as "wilderness," and 30 percent due to the arbitrary closing of access roads by the NPS. Just as with Virginia's displaced Shenandoah mountaineers, the Ozark river people found themselves locked away from their centuries-old private family cemeteries.

Little Leon Somerville ("Little" synonymous here with "Junior") of Cozahome, Arkansas, has waged a long-running battle on behalf of his confused and unorganized neighbors. Somerville worked for many years as a surveyor—at least five years with a private company on the BNR boundary. He speaks of seeing many homes and buildings "moved, dismantled or bulldozed." He estimates (conservatively) that "500 families lost their farms and/or homes, vacation cabins, businesses."

Somerville says trying to obtain accurate statistics is difficult because of the methods of record-keeping employed by the NPS. For example, mobile homes were not recognized as permanent residences, and Leon emphasizes, "There are *lots* of mobile homes here in the Ozarks." He says many families were "extended families," with several generations living and working the same farm. If your name was not on the property deed, then you didn't count—even if you'd lived there all your life.

More than two decades after the fact, Somerville says the whole thing is remembered as "a very bad time." He says most of the landowners were coerced through "threat of condemnation," and that they "felt intimidated." When the subject is approached today, Leon writes: "Everybody gets aggravated and mad as hell all over again. The men will be cussin' and the women will be crying. It is not a topic to be approached lightly."

The festering sore refuses to heal. Without regard for human rights or emotions, or conscience for past transgressions against American citizens, the Sierra Club began pressing Congress in mid-1993 to acquire from "willing landowners" as much as 840,000 additional acres comprising the entire Buffalo River watershed.

They want it all . . . and will go to extended limits to get it.

Donald Scott, a 61-year-old rancher near Malibu, California, didn't know the extent of those "limits" when he complained to NPS rangers that boulders from the Santa Monica National Recreation Area were being dumped on his Trail's End Ranch. NPS Superintendent David Gackenbach went personally to Scott's ranch with a six-pack of beer and an informal request to walk the property with its owner. Gackenbach later told the Malibu *Surfside News* he took advantage of an opportunity to see the ranch that was generally "off limits to the agency."

Scott's wife said her husband was known as a "heavy drinker" and an outspoken critic of government agencies.

On October 2, a dozen vehicles and two dozen officers—National Park Service police among them—raided the Trail's End Ranch, armed with guns and a warrant to search for 50 marijuana plants allegedly spotted from the air. Scott and his wife were wakened by loud voices and banging on the door. Recovering from cataract surgery, Scott took up a gun to protect himself and his wife. When confronted by armed officers and their orders to put his gun down, he moved to obey, and was instantaneously mowed down by several bullets to the chest.

No marijuana plants were ever found on the ranch.

Scott's attorney and old friend Nick Gutsue questions the presence of NPS rangers at the so-called "drug raid." Could NPS participation have been motivated by laws providing for the confiscation of property involved in drug-related violations? Or did NPS bureaucrats devise the whole scheme?

Some targeted victims of the NPS are now fighting back.

Ann Corcoran of Sharpsburg, Maryland, educated at Rutgers Agricultural College and Yale Forestry School, had worked for The Nature Conservancy and as a lobbyist for the National Audubon Society. She dreamed of owning a farm.

In 1985, Ann and her husband bought 160 acres near Antietam Battlefield National Park. They renovated their "homestead" and were just nicely settled in when they learned the National Park Service was planning to expand Antietam Park. Alarmed by the likelihood of finding their land enclosed within the new proposed boundaries, the Corcorans began checking and were told the expansion was needed because the area was being threatened with "unsightly commercial development."

Without informing local landowners, the NPS had asked a Nature Conservancy spinoff group to begin quietly acquiring the farms around Antietam. The land would then be transferred to the government in exchange for compensatory tax benefits.

The Corcorans were acquainted with inholders living within Antietam Park boundaries who enjoyed virtually no allowable use of their own land. Fearing similar restrictions on their farm, or perhaps even facing condemnation and the loss of their property, the Corcorans investigated further and found "no evidence whatsoever" that commercial development was forthcoming to the National Park perimeter. To avoid being surrounded by park expansion, they bought an additional 150 acres adjoining their farm that ran outside the new proposed park boundary.

They organized opposition rallies and town meetings to educate their neighbors, and generated media coverage. Property owners facing similar problems across the country began to respond and offer their support. Finally, the NPS put its plan for immediate expansion of Antietam National Park on a back burner. And while agency desires for enlarging Antietam may never die, the vigorous opposition efforts of Ann Corcoran and her supporters succeeded at least in delaying the action.

A similar battle is being fought by Alice Menks and her husband in Graves Mill, Virginia. They built a house in 1984 only to find out their lot had been designated for national park use in 1926 when Shenandoah National Park was formed. Some designated land had not been included in the original park boundary and was left to private ownership. But the Menks discovered the Conservation Fund was moving to secretly buy up more of the land and turn it over to the NPS. In self-defense, the Menks helped to organize a group called Virginians for Property Rights in 1991. Alice Menks says the NPS "treated us like naughty children," and their battle against park expansion continues.

Ann Corcoran, believing in the basic principles of freedom and having experienced federal bureaucrats' disregard for private property rights, became active in publishing _Land Rights Letter_—a strong and vigorous voice today for property rights advocates. Alice Menks joined Leri Thomas to produce a startling report on the subversive and coercive behavior of the NPS entitled _Us vs. NPS._

Greedy bureaucracies invariably commit gross mismanagement of their resources and programs. The NPS is no exception.

Tourists visiting Antietam Battlefield National Park in recent years reported sewage overflowing from septic tanks at the visitors' center. Neighbors living near Shenandoah National Park accuse the NPS of cutting down forests to relocate ranger stations when current facilities could have been renovated or replaced on the same sites. Catastrophic fires at Yellowstone have been blamed by forestry experts on the absence of planned management. And while NPS Director Roger Kennedy bemoans the state of disrepair at many of the 340 national parks, monuments and historic sites under his care, he boasts that acquiring and designating additional parks is on the Clinton Administration agenda.

They want it all—begged, bought, borrowed or stolen.

In October of 1993, at least 15 preservationist groups came together at the National Wildlife Federation's Laurel Ridge Center in Virginia. The purpose? To map out a war plan on property rights and to strategize on effective ways of shooting down legislation and court cases that appear to favor landowners. Part of the conference—(perhaps "seminar" is a better word)—dealt strictly with the strategy of "taking" private land by rendering it useless to the landowner through regulation, and thereby avoiding constitutional provisions for compensation.

These groups conspire to _steal_ private land—and they have the endorsement and support of federal bureaucrats!

The mind-set for this "takings coalition" is articulated in the September/October 1993 issue of _National Parks_—the official publication of the National Parks and Conservation Association. Author Richard Stapleton was completely comfortable propounding the absolute nonexistence of property rights. "Ownership . . . is temporal," he wrote, "the land belongs to none of us."

(If this is the case, who dreamed up property _taxes?_)

Stapleton continues: "From the first tenuous settlements that included village greens and commons, land use in America has historically been determined by, and in, the public interest. The right to do this or that on any given parcel of land is not inalienable; it has been given by the community, and it can be taken away by the community . . .

"We are learning, but it is a fight," Stapleton goes on, "a fight not just against the Wise Use Movement and its offspring, the Property Rights Movement, but against the belief that property is one of those inalienable rights endowed to us by our Creator through the Declaration of Independence."

(Folks, this is from the National Parks and Conservation Association! "Wise use" and "property rights," by their very definitions, should command respect. Observe here that, along with naked *disrespect* for our U.S. Constitution, the above terminologies are used as if they were the defilers of an otherwise perfect Earth.)

The subversive agendas of government bureaucracies were once kept secret and their covert operations low-key, but that's not the case anymore because the agencies (and agents within them) perceive themselves as being so powerful they no longer need to hide from or answer to the American public. For the most part, they're right. The American public has become so *civilized* that we *tolerate* incredible levels of inequity and injustice administered by those we *perceive* as being more powerful.

(A hundred years ago there was common law, and tar and feathers, too; the government was *not* taking anybody's land then.)

They want it all—and there's more than one way to get it.

An attractive envelope arrives in your mailbox. You unsheathe an innocuous-appearing letterhead and begin reading. The magniloquence is almost tranquilizing:

Dear Investor,
I'd like you to prepare yourself for a mild shock of a most rare and welcome kind.

There is indeed a group that has quietly "bought up" acres and acres of wild land in your state.

But not for condominiums or shopping centers, golf courses or industrial parks. Not for strip mining or timber cutting or highways or parking lots. Not for profit or private gain at all.

For love. For life. For the preservation of this exquisitely beautiful planet of ours. For the benefit of future generations of all its inhabitants . . .

Enter The Nature Conservancy (TNC).

TNC is a great-sounding organization with a great-sounding mission; they've fooled a lot of people, including farmers and ranchers and others clinging tenaciously to their own property rights. In reality, The Nature Conservancy is one of the most effective government "machines" in operation today, and its _true_ mission is to buy up the nation and turn it over to the various federal agencies for quick and handsome profits.

At any given time, TNC owns millions of acres of land across the U.S. This unique private preservationist group is the largest real estate broker in the country, buying about 1,000 acres everyday. In 1990, TNC's Trade Lands Program Director Richard Friedman told the 46th annual National Association of Home Builders Convention, "We have a portfolio of about 300 properties around the country we're marketing at any one time. We bring in about 100 pieces . . . a year from individuals and corporations."

The TNC's operating budget exceeds $125,000,000 a year. It's total assets are approaching $750,000,000. TNC is quite easily the wealthiest preservationist group in America. That, along with its affinity for quick, quiet and enormously profitable deals with NPS, FWS, BLM and others, makes TNC as dangerous as it is wealthy.

Humanitarianism is not the fire within this organization; quite simply, the motivator here is profit. Various government agencies heretofore mentioned consistently pay higher-than-market-value prices for land acquired by TNC, sometimes within a day or two of the TNC acquisition. In 1988 and '89, the Fish and Wildlife Service paid TNC $4,500,000 for about 5,400 acres in Oklahoma appraised at $3,500,000. That's a $1,000,000 gratuity paid with taxpayers' dollars.

Similar examples abound.

The Bureau of Land Management gave TNC $1,400,000 with which to purchase 5,529 acres in Oregon. The Conservancy had bought an option on the land for $100. The deal was completed with the landowner for $1,260,000, leaving TNC with $140,000 for a prearranged transaction.

In a 1992 report from the Inspector General of the DOI, the National Park Service was shown to have paid $4,770,000 for 4,200 acres in South Carolina on the strength of an appraisal done a year-and-a-half earlier—*before* the land was devastated by Hurricane Hugo!

Other "nonprofit" groups function on a smaller scale but just as effectively as TNC in acquiring land for transfer to federal agencies—the National Audubon Society, the Trust for Public Land, et cetera. In 1991 alone, three federal agencies within the DOI—Fish and Wildlife Service, National Park Service and Bureau of Land Management— spent nearly $220,000,000 to buy private lands. In the six fiscal years ending with 1991, the same three agencies expended $992,000,000 removing additional lands from private ownership and local tax rolls. Hundreds of these transactions were accomplished through the skilled manipulations of the "nonprofits." The IG's 1992 report cited 64 transactions in which the FWS alone paid more than $5,200,000 over fair market value to nonprofit organizations for private land acquisitions.

The practice, while unethical and deliberate—in some cases, probably illegal—is not about to stop or change much; the "nonprofits" like the profits, and federal bureaucrats like the ease with which they're able to acquire taxpayers' property with taxpayers' money. DOI Secretary Babbitt told the Natural Resources Committee in February of 1993 that he wholeheartedly approved of nonprofit groups acquiring lands and selling them profitably to the government.

A Fish and Wildlife Service manual on Fee Acquisition states: " . . . Federal agencies, have found advantages in employing intermediate private parties, such as a local chapter of The Nature Conservancy, in their fee acquisition program in order to soften the specter of 'big government' intervention."

(They *know* they're the "bad guys" . . . so they plot tactics and strategies to fool you.)

A 1990 Memorandum of Understanding (MOR) drawn between the BLM and The Nature Conservancy declares a "policy of cooperation and coordination" in authorizing TNC "to assist the BLM in the acquisition of privately owned land."

(Beginning to understand preservationist clout in bureaucratic circles . . ?)

They want it all—and where there's a will, there's a way.

The National Park Service has a contingency fund containing many millions of dollars for the sole purpose of acquiring private lands bordering existing parks. Additionally, the NPS's "National Natural and Historical Landmarks Program" is affecting as many as 90,000,000 acres of private property. The NPS created the program to designate lands with ecological values of national significance—another way of rendering private land useless to the landowner.

Alston Chase wrote in *The Washington Times* that, as a result of this program, " . . . officials secretly evaluated thousands of properties for landmark status, trespassed on private lands without permission and illegally designated hundreds as national landmarks without the owners' knowledge or consent." A report by the Inspector General said such designations " . . . could result in unwanted land use restrictions or other protective measures being imposed on the landowners . . . " The IG determined that more than " . . . 2,800 private landowners may have had their property rights infringed upon."

Is the NPS (or the DOI) intimidated by such a report?

The program continues while Congress has inflated the National Natural Landmarks budget from less than $200,000 to more than $1,000,000. Eric Veyhl, Chairman of the Maine Conservation Rights Institute, believes the Landmark evaluation process is a "feeder program" used to justify land acquisition by the federal government. While official claims of "national significance" are used to restrict or block private land use, NPS preservationists lobby Congress for more funds to acquire the land. Then, of course, there's the National Heritage Conservation Act allowing direct governmental control over sites designated as "significant."

There are many more such programs, agencies, commissions and trusts poised to take possession of the private lands in America. There are National Preserves, National Heritage Programs, National Forests, National Riparian Conservation Areas, National Recreation Areas and National Wildlife Refuges. Not to be out-done by any of its sister groups, the National Trust for Historic Preservation listed the *entire state of Vermont* as one of its 11 "Most Endangered Historic Places" in 1993.

Incidentally, the National Trust for Historic Preservation was created by Congress in 1949, and actually has an appropriated budget allowing it to run amuck with this kind of preservation-rooted lunacy. Property owners are the victims.

The federal agencies and their respective "responsible" bureaucrats insist that efforts to enlarge the national parks and refuges, conservation areas and "public" lands in general, are pursued only through private landowners *willing* to sell. Many former property owners, having dealt with agents of the federal government, disagree.

Bo Thott of the Washington County Alliance in Maine used the Freedom of Information Act to obtain the names and addresses of 1,130 people who had sold their private land to the National Park Service in the year preceding September 30, 1992.

(Even that number within that time frame is alarming.)

Thott heard from over 400 of these so-called "willing sellers" in response to his inquiry about the "voluntary" nature of their transactions. Well over 25 percent of these said they did not sell out willingly. Nearly three-fourths of the respondents to the survey recalled threats of condemnation of their properties if they did not sell.

An Arizona seller wrote: "It's hard to buck the government so I sold."

Someone in Ohio explained: " . . . we were told . . . we had no choice."

A New York respondent said: "We had no intention of selling. I was told I had to."

These and many more responses collected by Thott are the typical symptom of an American public grown so tolerant of a government perceived to be all-powerful that coercion, in many cases, comes in the form of diplomacy—or the tactful and sympathetic delivery of "bad news." The American people have been schooled in the art of swallowing bureaucratic abuses and left to believe they "had no choice."

(It's been said a true bureaucrat is the person who can tell you to go to hell, and make you look forward to the trip.)

Hence, property owners are losing their lands to federal acquisition efforts at the pace of about 1,000 acres a day—want to or not, like it or otherwise.

Dean Kleckner, President of the American Farm Bureau Federation, says, "The right to own and use property, guaranteed by the Constitution, is as important as the right to worship, to free speech, to vote . . . The federal government is vigilant in its defense of other civil rights and liberties— why shouldn't the right to own and use property enjoy the same status? The Fifth Amendment says it should."

Ultimately, American landowners will decide if it will.

The freedoms, rights and powers granted sovereign individuals by the Constitution and Bill of Rights are still in effect. The American public must only realize it is not subservient to an omnipotent array of federal bureaucracies. In fact, it is all very much the other way around. The *people* have the power. However, much of that power is tied directly to the free pursuits of individual destinies, the right to elect or terminate government representatives, the unrestricted ownership and use of private property.

Federal bureaucracies and the government which creates them know better than anyone where they stand—the actions allowed them, the limited powers granted them, the restrictions placed on them by the founders of this nation. Their actions are not by accident, but rather by design. Communitarian governments around the world have demonstrated that to own or control the land is to own and control the people.

They want it all—and they'll have it, too, if the American people don't stand up and exercise their constitutional rights while some of them still exist.

V. **The Noetic Obsession**

There is a "religion" among us with many names, and yet no name at all. It has been called pantheism, animism, inhumanism, organicism, mysticism, transcendentalism, and any number of other elusively descriptive tags. Regardless of who calls it what, it possesses one basic central tenet; it espouses wilderness worship.

It is the noetic obsession.

Three prominent conservationists of more than a century ago have been credited with fostering the creation of a sentiment akin to worshiping the earth. John Muir, founder of the Sierra Club and recognized today as the "father of modern environmentalism," proudly proclaimed that nature was his "religion." He wrote to naturist poet Ralph Waldo Emerson, " . . . join me in a month's worship with Nature in the high temples . . . beyond our holy Yosemite . . . in the name of all the spirit creatures of these rocks and of this whole spiritual atmosphere . . . "

Emerson—a former Unitarian minister—who had long before abandoned Christianity, and researched and rejected both Buddhism and Judaism, joined with Muir in his spiritual communion with the wilderness. He brought with him Henry David Thoreau, who truly believed that "Nature" was a synonym for "God." In his previous writings, Thoreau had declared his faith in the "immortality of a pine tree." In the heralded classic *Walden*, he had denounced all that promoted civilization and modern development. In 1862, he penned the motto of the twentieth-century preservationist movement: "In wildness is the preservation of the world."

Alston Chase, respected scholar and columnist, wrote in his book _Playing God In Yellowstone: The Destruction of America's First National Park_: "Theirs was an eclectic faith of the wilderness. Emerson was its Moses, leading the faithful out of the grasp of established religion; Thoreau its Isaiah, the prophet; and Muir its David, guardian of the Promised Land."

Other renowned individuals have since subscribed to their noetic doctrines—Charles Lindbergh, the aviator; William O. Douglas, outspoken environmentalist and jurist on the U.S. Supreme Court; Ansel Adams, world-famous photographer and conservationist; and Joseph Wood Krutch, drama critic and outdoor writer for the _New York Times_.

Names and personalities such as these—some regarded as American heroes and crusaders in other causes—lent credibility and respectability to a movement built on a philosophy of transcendentalism. In his later works, Emerson held fast to a belief that a godlike spirit inhabited all things, and that Nature was the symbol of the spirit.

Other American writers of the period subscribed almost unwittingly to the philosophy. Garrett Hardin's _The Tragedy of the Commons_ and William Kittredge's _Owning It All_ berated the so-called _laissez-faire_ attitude attached to the unrestricted use of water, rangeland and wildlife.

The actual embodiment of the noetic obsession materialized in late 1966 when a professor of history at the University of California, Lynn White, Jr., addressed the American Association for the Advancement of Science in Washington, D.C. White declared without equivocation that Judeo-Christianity was destroying the world. By some logic—perhaps contrived by White to create controversy or attract notice during a restless social period—the professor reasoned that Christianity had destroyed pagan animism thereby making it possible " . . . to exploit nature in a mood of indifference to the feelings of natural objects."

(This is a university-level professor of history ennobling the _feelings of natural objects!_)

White alleged this rape of nature came directly as the result of biblical directives to "subdue the earth."

Consequently, western Christian cultures supposedly took aim at the world of nature, bent on its destruction as a road to civil and industrial development.

Chase wrote in *Yellowstone* the environmental movement was about to stumble over itself after two decades of political victories prior to White's address. With Congress having enacted most of its agenda into law, Chase asked, " .. where would environmentalists go from here?"

Professor White cast them the noetic hook and, like hungry fish, they took the bait. Timing could not have been more perfect. Some environmentalists without another definite direction were quick to grasp this new crutch. It gave them purpose and inspiration. Predominant cultures and customs rooted in Christianity would all be targeted as the black-hearted villains of the natural world.

Subscribers to the philosophy are unabashedly fanatical (if not radical), and their "religion" itself borders on the occult. Like most other religions, however, noeticism itself has been corrupted by newer generations not fully comprehending its concept; Muir, Emerson and Thoreau were probably its only true purists. Contemporary high-profile noetic "evangelists" include Aldo Leopold, founder of the Wilderness Society, and David Brower, longtime president of the Sierra Club and founder of Friends of the Earth. Dr. Willis Harmon, a cofounder of the Institute of Noetic Sciences (yes, there really is such a place), talks loudly about "connecting our social, spiritual and ecological visions," and about reinventing the world.

Al Gore, while serving as a U.S. Senator from Tennessee, wrote in his book *Earth in Balance* that humanity can only be saved, physically and emotionally, by a "spiritual relationship with Earth."

Ron Arnold, Chairman of the Center for the Defense of Free Enterprise, located in Bellevue, Washington, is quite probably the man most feared by radical eco-preservationists. The reason? He is educated, articulate, brilliant and fearless. He comes from inside their ranks, and they know he's seen inside their heads, examined their motives, is not deluded by their social deviations. A one-time Sierra Club official, Arnold welcomes head-on dialogue with his former colleagues—something most of them strive to avoid. In 1992, Arnold told the Boston *Globe*, "Environmentalism is the new paganism. Trees are worshiped and humans are sacrificed at its altar . . . It is evil . . . and we intend to destroy it."

Property owners and users of other lands—and all American citizens who believe in the virtues of the U.S. Constitution and Bill of Rights—should be advised that the battle of which Arnold speaks will not be an easy one. Those esteemed documents were drawn from the convictions of men who had known government oppression and understood the meaning of feudalism. Noetic pantheists comprise only one of numerous battalions dedicated now to challenging (and eliminating, if possible) the principles of good and right, humanity and freedom, and most basic civil rights.

VI. Visions and Strategies

It cannot be said that the preservationist movement is weak. Neither are the preservationists themselves without dedication. Their visions and ambitions—their strategies for assaulting property rights and land use—were allowed several quiet decades to become refined and firmly entrenched before very much notice was given them. Their public agendas seemed so unreproachable. Quixotic legislation was passed in support of their programs because, at the time, their ideals appeared beneficial to humanity, wildlife and the environment as a whole. Widespread public opinion was favorable because few had begun to ferret out the vipers in the grass, and expose the hidden dangers of what was really happening.

Noeticism, preservationist zeal, bureaucratic greed, power-lust and ignorance are all important players in the assault on "inalienable rights" as we were taught from children to know them. This is not a minor skirmish with a single battleline drawn; it is an all-out war with many fronts, and every attack coming in waves.

(Warfare analysts have speculated that Custer's 7th Cavalry might have won the Battle of Little Bighorn had the enemy not continued to materialize in assault after assault from so many different directions.)

Attacks on property ownership, land use and resource harvest are embodied in wetlands determinations, the Endangered Species Act, critical habitat designations, national parks and wildlife refuges, rangeland and mining law reform, wild and scenic rivers designations, the preservation of historic sites, national natural landmarks, and other preservationist causes too numerous to list within the confines of a single paragraph. The point is: the assault is unending, with a new and larger wave following each one before.

Uninformed idealists are almost as dangerous as the obsessed environmental strategists. Case in point: New York Congresswoman Carolyn Maloney (the same one who thinks they don't use much metal in New York) sponsored the Northern Rockies Ecosystem Protection Act in 1994, attempting to consign 13,000,000 acres in five western states to "wilderness" status. It didn't take long for Maloney to pick up about four dozen *eastern* cosponsors. Idaho Congressman Larry LaRocco referred to the bill as "radical" and said he's tired of " . . . eastern environmentalists trying to tell westerners what's best for their region."

The environmental offensive is not being applied by happenstance; it is part of a very carefully plotted strategy designed to win the war by deliberate and persistent onslaught. The two newest and biggest weapons in the preservationists' arsenal were looming on the horizon in 1993—the National Biological Survey and the Wildlands Project.

The NBS is an ambitious project fostered by DOI Secretary Babbitt, and introduced for him in Congress by more than one representative *of the people*—one of them being Congressman Gerry Studds of Massachusetts. According to Jay Hair, President of the National Wildlife Federation, the survey will ultimately produce a " . . . map . . . showing . . . major types of vegetation . . . across the

United States, and the types and numbers of animals, birds, fish and . . . insects that live or migrate within the ecosystems . . . " Language in the Biological Survey Act of 1993 would authorize federal agencies to catalog, then formulate a plan to protect, all plant and animal life within the United States.

(Anyone recalling the effects of Endangered Species legislation should be horrified.)

The Wildlands Project is the brainchild of Dave Foreman, founder of the militant environmentalist group Earth First! The project has drafted a mission statement and formulated a radical plan to "re-wild" all of the North American continent. A part of that plan calls for placing half of the conterminous United States off-limits to humanity, while the remaining half would be habitat for human population—that, too, strictly regulated. The left-leaning media and noted scientists alike are giving the Wildlands concept more and more attention—and respectability.

The mentality behind these two grandiloquent schemes is verbalized by Jerry Rogers, a former assistant director of cultural resources for the National Park Service: " . . . the greatest threat to . . . natural resources . . . comes not from federal agencies, but from private parties doing private things on private land."

(Our Constitution guarantees us the _right_ to do private things on private land!)

The basic difference between Babbitt and Foreman is: Babbitt wants to _control_ the land by controlling the people, and Foreman wants to _eliminate_ the human element altogether. _Both_ their plans are being given serious consideration.

Let's look at them individually.

Secretary Babbitt has been espousing the virtues of "land-based" wildlife management as opposed to the "species-based" approach for some time. There is no variation here from his belief in "ecosystem management" and other "communitarian" attitudes toward land use and property ownership. Enactment of the NBS would allow federal agents and their assistants (mostly volunteers from preservationist groups like Sierra Club, Friends of the Earth, and Earth First!) to trespass on private land while gathering data. Federal law would prevent landowners from interfering with these "surveyors." Further, property owners would not be allowed access to the data collected on their lands—even through the Freedom of Information Act. Literally, a farmer could be forbidden from cultivating his fields and never given a reason more specific than " . . . your land is environmentally sensitive." Even more frightening, low-ranking regional bureaucrats would be writing determinations and enforcing restrictions with no provision for review or appeal.

The National Biological Survey will become another division of the already-enormous DOI bureaucracy—complete with director and regional offices. It will be the arm of federal government (with congressional blessing) that effectively destroys land use and ownership as heretofore recognized in the United States. Already, the National Wildlife Federation and The Nature Conservancy are beginning to talk about enormous "bioreserves," and controlling human activity to protect plant and animal species.

John Lancaster of the *Washington Post* writes, "The idea is to manage public and private lands not as isolated fragments, but as integrated parts of a much larger whole.."

(The plan is to manage *private* lands!)

If the desire to prevent Americans from making decisions affecting their own private properties was not the ultimate objective of the NBS, then why didn't Bruce Babbitt allow it to be passed into law in 1993 with a couple of protective property rights amendments attached? Babbitt and his friends from the environmental groups had lobbied vigorously against any kind of amendments, and when some astute congressmen (especially Hayes from Louisiana and Taylor from North Carolina) rallied support for protection of private property owners, Babbitt pulled the legislation.

American landowners are not necessarily out of the woods on this one. Contrary to the normal process of things, the U.S. House and Senate had already appropriated a total of $321,000,000 for the NBS, and, confident the authorization would pass, Babbitt staffed the new agency and appointed its first deputy director. The Secretary perceives himself as unstoppable, and will proceed with or without congressional approval—unless someone shuts him down.

That *someone* is not likely to care about the subversive and conspiratorial behavior of the Secretary of the Interior. He put him there. The agenda of Bruce Babbitt is the agenda of Bill Clinton, Al Gore, George Frampton, Jack Ward Thomas and others. The Clinton Administration has packed the executive branch with staunch eco-activists, and top-level Clinton appointees have been instructed to hire more environmentalists to their staffs.

Syndicated columnist William Kramer writes: " . . . they don't want anyone using federal lands for any reason . . . Emboldened by an administration which supports their agendas, green fanatics are marching. Some want 26,000,000 acres of northeastern forests barred to public use. Some want the Mississippi made an enormous park. Most worship nature and condemn humans."

After a vicious battle in 1993 over grazing fees on western rangelands was dead-ended by a Senate filibuster, Babbitt announced he would modify his plan for tighter restrictions, and allow more flexibility with local ranchers, environmentalists and public officials. This was not a magnanimous gesture on the part of the Secretary—not when *all* grazing could be stopped by implementation of the National Biological Survey!

Secretary Babbitt is a brilliant and dangerously manipulative bureaucrat. Property owners and land users are learning quickly that when he smiles, offers a handshake or a compromise, it is not without serving a purpose for the Secretary. He has stated publicly that he was "born to be Secretary of the Interior," and his environmental agenda is so inflexible that he rejected an opportunity to sit on the U.S Supreme Court for the rest of his life when Justice Harry Blackmun retired in April of 1994. He says he's glad he no longer has to answer to a constituency of voters. His is a constituency of one—President Clinton—and only the *President's* fear of voter sentiment will precipitate a change at the Interior Department.

Babbitt and Dave Foreman share a similar attitude of self-machismo; their illusions of grandeur lend themselves to visions of colossal amplitude.

Foreman pitched his newest "apocalypse" in Tempe, Arizona, during the summer of 1993. For more than ten years he had fostered and assembled fragments of the plan. Even supportive environmentalists initially said it was too wild to warrant serious consideration.

Called the North American Wilderness Recovery Project—otherwise known as Wildlands—the project detailed the restoration of entire landscapes. A system of connected wilderness reserves would crisscross the continent, displacing human inhabitants, closing roads, dismantling dams, removing powerlines, reclaiming developed farms and whole communities. The reserves would be decided by the omnipotence of plants and animals, with absolute disregard for economies, the human environment, spectacular scenery or recreational opportunities.

Foreman said all existing national parks, wildlife refuges and other sanctuaries would be abandoned in deference to the larger reserves and their more effective means for ecosystem management. He said, "Our goal is to create a new political reality based on the needs of other species."

(Some media, scientists *and* politicians are taking this guy seriously, folks! How much of your tolerance level is left?)

Reed Noss, a conservation biologist from Corvallis, Oregon, fully endorses the whole idea. He says, as one example, a study of grizzly bears shows that 50 bears require about 12,000,000 acres to adequately roam, forage and breed. A thousand grizzlies, then, would require 242,000,000 acres. Noss suggests accomplishing this by connecting the Greater Yellowstone Ecosystem with the Northern Continental Divide Ecosystem, *and* with the Canadian Rockies. The area would be off-limits to humans and stripped of human artifacts. Supporters of the Wildlands Project are talking about " bio*regions*," now—a step up from bioreserves.

Is Foreman's vision too radical to worry about? Not for a minute. One must only observe the evolution of the environmental movement to comprehend the imminent danger. No one would have believed the National Park Service would displace families with guns and handcuffs, and bulldoze and burn their homes. Who could have predicted the nightmares resulting from wetlands and endangered species protection? Wild and Scenic Rivers legislation allows property owners to remain on their land only for 25 years, or until the death of the owner (that could be tomorrow). No one may inherit or continue to use the land. Remember, Congress approved funding for the National Biological Survey before there *was* a National Biological Survey. Nothing is learned from past mistakes.

A blatant disregard for the rights of American property owners—and the basic civil right of "owning" land, as guaranteed us by our founding fathers—runs rampant in Washington. There are so many personal agendas disguised by misleading rhetoric and the carefully crafted language of legislation. *EcoScam* author Ron Bailey says, "Ecological alarmists are very skilled at manufacturing 'crises' that prompt congressional response." He points out that 450 national environmental organizations—some with household names like Audubon and Greenpeace—are funded by misled memberships numbering in the millions. The top ten alone raise most of half-a-billion dollars a year. Bailey says, "That buys a *lot* of influence in Washington, D.C."

It is not a wise man, either, who becomes so preoccupied with the big guns that he forgets there are literally hundreds of smaller organizations with equally ambitious objectives. The desperate and vindictive nature of most of them is epitomized by the little-known Oregon Natural Desert Association. The ONDA filed a lawsuit in U.S. District Court in Portland in May of 1994, claiming that grazing cattle along the John Day River in the Malheur National Forest had destroyed vegetation and caused the temperature of the river to rise. ONDA leader Bill Marlett promised to use the same argument to challenge grazing on 320,000,000 acres of federal land if the John Day lawsuit is successful. (Equally as ludicrous, it's a provision of the Clean Water Act empowering states to *set temperature standards for rivers* that has allowed this to happen.)

A groundswell of grassroots resistance to environmental overkill and bureaucratic steamrolling is beginning to make itself known. The Sierra Club—famous for its ongoing volley of lawsuits—is itself being sued by the victims of environmental zeal. Property rights groups, organizations representing western interests, and local governments are calling for the resignation or dismissal of

DOI Secretary Babbitt. Chambers of commerce are engaging in letter-writing campaigns on political issues. Some western governors have threatened to sue the U.S. Government on behalf of their states' residents.

But the American public must do more.

The attitude that "someone else will do it for me" is synonymous today with "go ahead and do it to me." While high-dollar eco-organization lobbyists may entertain the politicians and buy their television ads, their numbers are small when compared to American voters. Homeowners (even renters) who don't want NBS volunteers trampling through their yards, fields and rose gardens should contact every congressman available. Solicitous letters from benign-sounding groups aspiring to preserve some idyllic landscape should be summarily burned.

The power of America still rests with its people—not with the politicians, the bureaucrats, the preservationists or their lobbyists. As long as the American public is willing to tolerate the political inequities, to accept the abuses, to pay the tab—to "roll over and play dead"—the compounding of injustices will continue. Without a resisting voice from the "silent majority," the National Biological Survey could very quickly become a fact of life, with the Wildlands Project close on its heels.

Are these the embodiment of our destinies?

VII. **A Push for Centralized Control**

Many political "movements" and world events indicate a growing sentiment favoring centralized international government. Most notably, armed troops from an array of nations converge on some remote troubled region like Bosnia or Somalia and serve under United Nations command. Worldwide and international trade agreements are negotiated, all directed primarily toward relaxing or dissolving border restrictions. Within our own country, additional gun control (another erosion of constitutional rights), the breakdown of the military (at the risk of our national defense), and the push for socialized medicine (which doesn't work anywhere else in the world), are all bright orange flags warning of the dangers just ahead.

Prior to the 1992 election of Bill Clinton and Al Gore to the White House, Mountain States Legal Foundation Chief Council William Perry Pendley wrote in _Blue Ribbon Magazine_: "Gore advocates adoption of a 'Global Marshall Plan' under which the free market system, having demonstrated its superiority over communism, 'must undergo a profound transformation.' Thus, having won a stunning victory over totalitarianism, we must now surrender meekly to green tyranny."

The article goes on to describe how Gore would require U.S. citizens to fund massive programs here and abroad through a host of new taxes. He would allow development of only "environmentally appropriate" technologies, and would enter into international agreements to be enforced by a new _United Nations_ "Stewardship Council."

(William Pendley did not make this up; Al Gore did.)

Vice President Gore has little faith in human technology. In his own writings he has declared, "We are not that clever, and never have been." He uses this logic as justification for _government_—both national and _inter_national—to decide what technologies are "appropriate," what economic progress would be allowable under the New Order, and to predetermine the economies and lives and destinies of the people. Gore says this nation has "tilted" too far in the past toward "individual rights," and his vision of centralized control will fix all that.

Visionaries such as Gore and Clinton are extremely dangerous men. They aligned themselves in such a way with the American public that they were able to attain political status (and office) that is only a means to a further end. Look at what happened. Within a matter of months from the 1992 election, the Natural Resources Secretary for the Tri-Lateral Commission and former President of the League of

Conservation Voters was appointed Secretary of the Interior; the President of the Wilderness Society was made *Assistant* Secretary of the Interior; a New Mexico public lands commissioner and board member of the Wilderness Society was named Director of the Bureau of Land Management; and the Oregon wildlife biologist who led the "scientific" team advising President Clinton with misinformation about northern spotted owls became Chief of the Forest Service.

The system of western democratic government is eroding, as surely as are the "inalienable rights" guaranteed by it. The primary reason is: many high political offices are held by individuals who do not respect or believe in the basic principles of the system. The Clinton Administration is permeated with radicals of that persuasion. Author Ron Bailey says, " . . . the radicals are distrustful of democratic politics. In a democracy, people generally look out for their own interests—which often aren't the agendas of the alarmists. That's why they prefer multinational organizations—the United Nation's Commission on Environment and Development, Earth Summit, and similar groups which essentially are beyond the reach of voters."

Former Washington Governor Dixy Lee Ray, property rights activist and ex-chairwoman of the Atomic Energy Commission, said those involved in the environmental movement " . . . don't like people very well." Speaking before the Arizona Private Property Rights Coalition, Ray concluded: " . . . they believe that we in the western world—particularly industrialized society—are not living on the earth the right way, and they're going to make us change. They truly believe in centralized government, central control—control of the behavior of people through legislation—and worst of all, they . . . would have us give up our own nation to come under the New World Order of a single world government under the United Nations."

The United Nations Covenant on Civil and Political Rights is a frightening document that has been kept mostly out of public scrutiny. However, by way of chronology, the U.N. Covenant was first introduced in 1966, but was not ratified. President Carter tried again for ratification in 1979, but failed. In 1991, President Bush again brought the document before the Senate. It was elevated to ratification in

August of that year, then passed without a recorded vote on April 2, 1992.

The Covenant is a direct salvo on the belief that certain "inalienable rights" come from the Creator and cannot be revoked. The document asserts that these "rights" shall be controlled " . . . in accordance with such procedures as are established by the (international) law." The Creator and the Constitution have been removed from the process. The U.N. Covenant is born of the warped idea that the omnipotence of government supersedes all individual rights.

Ratification of the Covenant has been kept quiet, the vote unrecorded and secret; the document has been laid carefully away. But the groundwork has now been laid for much more vigorous movement in the same direction at a later time.

The destruction or elimination of inalienable rights is as important to achieving a system of centralized control—or world government—as the meltdown of the Iron Curtain. Environmental power mongers view private property owners managing their own acreages with as much disdain as they did despotic tyrants controlling their republics from behind impenetrable national boundaries.

Wayne Hage (whom you'll come to know much better in the next chapter of this book), Nevada rancher and author of _Storm Over Rangelands_, has written eloquently about the philosophy of "inalienable rights." The following paragraphs are his:

"To understand what has happened to inalienable rights, we must look at the philosophy upon which inalienable rights were based. Law is the expression of fundamental belief. Statute sets forth the criteria of how the law is to be applied. In our system the Declaration of Independence is the basic philosophical expression of the nation's law. The Constitution tells us how the philosophy expressed in the Declaration of Independence is to be applied. As every school child knows—or at least they did in past generations—the Declaration of Independence is premised on inalienable rights.

"This is apparent in the opening lines of the Declaration of Independence: 'We hold these truths to be self-evident that all men are created equal and are endowed by their Creator with certain inalienable rights . . . '

"Did you notice that? The authors of the Declaration of Independence believed that inalienable rights were granted to man by their Creator. Thomas Jefferson and his associates who lent their beliefs to the writing of the Declaration of Independence believed a God existed. They had no problem acknowledging God as the Creator.

"These men were products of the period of enlightenment. To them, learning and truth were the foundation of all progress. They believed the new nation they were creating was a continuation of human progress. They were distancing themselves from the superstition and ignorance of the dark ages. They were glad to discard the myriad of theories handed down over millennia that life had generated spontaneously from such sources as ocean slime, mud banks off the coast of Greece, and old rags that turned into mice.

"They believed in law that was superior to the laws of men and men's governments. They believed that for law to be effective in governing a society it had to conform to the higher law of God.

"They believed that all men had the God-given right to life, liberty, and the pursuit of happiness. If a power higher than the laws and government of man had granted these rights, then no government of man had the prerogative to take or alienate these rights. Hence, we had inalienable rights. The natural extension of this belief was that if these inalienable rights were granted by a power higher than the governments of men, men were justified in opposing governments who attempted to take those rights. This was the basis for the American Revolution against Great Britain.

"Conversely, it follows, if there is no Creator, if there is no God who can grant rights to men, then men and their governments are the highest source of authority. If the governments of men are the highest authority, it follows that the privileges granted by man and man's governments can be revoked by man and man's government. There is no court of last resort. There is no appeal to a higher power. There are no inalienable rights.

"The reason inalienable rights seem to have disappeared from our nation's system of jurisprudence is because the basic philosophy upon which the concept of inalienable rights were based has all but disappeared.

"It may be that modern day American society has outgrown the concept of God. It may be that belief in some form of spontaneous generation of life is more acceptable than the simple belief in a Creator. But if we are to accept the premise that there is no creator, we also have to accept the fact that the basis for inalienable rights is also nonexistent."

Only the hearts and minds (and actions) of the American public can choose the way. Will our destinies be dictated by the continued erosion of freedoms and rights, and the ultimate shift to totalitarian control . . . or will it be a fierce dedication to a belief in and defense of inalienable rights?

The choice is yours.

V:

CANDLES IN
THE CAVERN

I. The Fight for Vested Rights

The American Dream is not lost to those who are willing to fight for it . . . and a lot of good citizens are fighting. Each one is a ray of hope—a lighted candle showing the way—for others just learning the nature of the battle.

Wayne and Jean Hage are consummate examples of the kind of courageous individuals leading the offensive to preserve the American way of life, its customs and cultures, its very basis for the freedoms and privileges most Americans have come to take for granted.

Wayne and Jean Hage *know* the nature of the battle.

For 14 years their battle on the Nevada Pine Creek Ranch was ongoing with the U.S. Forest Service. At first, it seemed perhaps coincidental that Forest Service officials would encourage Hage's cattle into "trespass" areas, then cite the Hages for trespass. It became a bit more obvious when unfounded charges were brought in order to cripple Hage's cattle operation, causing it to border on economic infeasibility. In a single 105-day grazing period during 1982, the Hages received 70 visits and 40 letters from Forest Service personnel, alleging violations that required quick and expensive responses.

It was apparent to Wayne Hage—a responsible and educated rancher in his mid-50s, holder of a master's degree in livestock management, and former board member of the Mountain States Legal Foundation—that federal bureaucrats were trying to force him to relinquish his property rights. In 1989, Hage wrote *Storm Over Rangelands* (described in *The Washington Post* as "part diatribe and part historical treatise"), accusing government and other interests of an orchestrated attack on the private property rights of westerners whose livelihoods depend on access to federal lands.

The Pine Creek Ranch encompasses 7,000 acres of deeded land, and an additional 240,000 acres in grazing allotments in the Toiyabe National Forest and 512,000 acres on Bureau of Land Management land. The Hages had run 2,000 head of cattle on these 759,000 acres until they sold most of their herd due to mounting costly restrictions and regulations.

In midsummer of 1991, Forest Service personnel armed with automatic rifles came and confiscated the remaining 100 head of Hage's livestock. Government officials justified their actions by claiming "resource damage"—the only legitimate excuse for reducing or canceling a grazing permit.

Hage believes it was more a case of collusion between the Forest Service, some members of Congress and national environmental groups who were angry about his book, and who wish to see cattle-grazing on unappropriated lands ended altogether. An independent range expert has since referred to the Meadow Canyon Allotment (where the cattle were confiscated) as "the best piece of range in the state of Nevada," and a Forest Service official admitted under oath that their actions were strictly punitive.

On September 26, 1991, Wayne and Jean Hage filed a $28,400,000 lawsuit in U.S. Claims Court against the Forest Service for the "taking" of their entire ranch through regulations and physical appropriation of property. The case involves federal lands, grazing allotments, water rights, private deeded land, and property in the form of cattle.

The Hages aroused the interests of two impressive San Francisco attorneys—Thomas Hookano and Mark Pollot, authors of the controversial Takings Executive Order while employed in the Reagan Administration—and some interesting twists have since materialized.

The suit was filed in *U.S. Claims Court* in Washington.

Hage says, "When you go to federal District Court, you are not . . . as we were taught in school, innocent until proven guilty. Federal District Court is there to protect the interests of the government. You are guilty until proven innocent. The federal District Court is not a common law court . . . "

The Claims Court is something quite different. Hage adds, "The Claims Court _is_ a common law court. You are able to get behind the government shield from discovery, which is called the Administrative Appeals process—there to protect the government from you the citizen."

In Claims Court, the defendant (in this case, the Forest Service) must comply with "full disclosure." Margaret Gabbard, Executive Director of the Free Enterprise Legal Defense Fund, writes: "Eighty-two years of ghosts, many of which have long been forgotten, are surfacing through subpoenas, document searches and depositions taken in the _Hage_ case. These documents show a clear trail of illegal activities between the Forest Service, other land management agencies, and preservationist organizations."

Hage points out, "This is the first time in history . . . that the Forest Service has ever been thrown into discovery . . . and the Forest Service—and the government as a whole— is desperate to stop this case."

Gabbard says, "This is the first opportunity that westerners have had to weed out those in agencies who are linked to the preservationist organizations, and who are forcing their agendas on the American public."

Within the unusual processes undergone in _Hage vs. United States_, the Nevada State Attorney General was forced to defend her hiring of National Wildlife Federation attorney Tom Lustig to represent the state in an attempt to intervene in the _Hage_ case on behalf of the Federal Government. Lustig asserted in court that he represented the "entire state of Nevada." Numerous state agencies have unequivocally denied any association with Lustig whatsoever.

Says Gabbard, "The attorney general placed the fate of an issue greatly affecting the entire western states in the hands of an organization (National Wildlife Federation) which certainly does not have the states' best interest in mind."

Further, electronic messages and other documentation have surfaced showing Robert Williamson, Head of Range Science for the Department of Agriculture, as having been kept apprised of the plans to confiscate Hage's cattle (originally planned to draw support for a hike in grazing fees on _all_ western public lands). Congressmen Mike Synar of

Oklahoma and Bruce Vento of Minnesota (both staunch anti-grazing legislators) also were kept informed about efforts to eliminate the Pine Creek Ranch.

Hage and his attorneys have never argued the premise that the Federal Government has the right to limit grazing activities on federally controlled land; they contend, rather, that such limitations trample on "preexisting rights"—on the vested interests—of ranchers and others whose presence and activities on the land *predate* the creation of forest reserves and their regulating agencies.

Attorney Mark Pollot argues that the grazing permit is a recognition of preexisting rights created by the investments of ranchers in the federal range. He said in court, " . . . while the grazing permit may be a privilege granted by Congress and therefore revocable, the water and grazing rights were created by local law and custom, and the blood and sweat of the early settlers. These underlying rights are not created by government and are not revocable by government without compensation."

Hage has challenged an obvious federal administrative double standard: while federal land managers call grazing permits "a privilege," revocable by the regulating bureaucracy, the Internal Revenue Service treats them as taxable "property."

It has been shown that the Pine Creek Ranch has contributed $120,000,000 to the local economy since the time it was settled. The Hages have never argued that the government should not have "taken" their ranching operation—such an argument would not be allowed in *Claims* Court. They simply demand compensation for what they've lost—$28,400,000.

Wayne Hage quips, "Any time a thief has to pay for what he steals, he soon loses his enthusiasm for stealing it."

Federal regulatory agencies, power-driven bureaucrats and ambitious preservationists have kept close eyes of *Hage vs. United States.* The outcome could dramatically affect a broad spectrum of government regulations and environmental projects impacting property (and vested) rights.

Everyone seems to be in agreement on that point.

"It's ultimately a question of who gets to control and use the resource," said Mark Pollot.

Tom Lustig said if Hage should win a monetary settlement, then federal lands managers would be reluctant to limit logging or mining or grazing on the lands they manage for fear of triggering similar lawsuits.

Wayne Hage could not agree more. "Their assessment of that is exactly right," he said. "That's exactly the way it should be."

By early 1994, a decision in *Hage* was still pending the submission of a report on a Nevada water rights adjudication, which government lawyers claimed would affect the case.

The final ruling could topple toward either side of the fence. Preservationists are not heartened by the Supreme Court ruling in *David H. Lucas vs. South Carolina Coastal Council*, favoring plaintiff Lucas to the tune of $1,200,000 for the loss of his right to develop a couple of beachfront lots.

Property rights advocates and other traditional users of government-claimed lands are encouraged that *Hage* has been argued before Claims Court Chief Judge Loren Allen Smith, who ruled in the 1990 case of *Loveladies Harbor Inc. vs. United States* that a landowner was due $2,600,000 from the federal government for being prevented from developing a wetland, and in *Whitney Benefits Inc. vs. United States* awarded $150,000,000 to a company barred by the Interior Department from mining coal in Wyoming.

Wayne and Jean Hage have lighted the path for other western lands users to defend and protect their private and vested property rights. *Hage vs. U.S.*, regardless of its outcome, can only represent the first volley of an offensive that must be taken up by persecuted ranchers and miners and communities and industries across the nation.

Hage says, "On this federal lands issue, we are dealing with the biggest scam ever perpetrated in this country since at least the Teapot Dome scandal of the 1920s."

He advises, "These are pivotal times in which we live. We need to be informed and . . . we need to have the courage to step out and take action."

In conclusion, Hages sets the tone for the long battle ahead. "The opposition is not playing games, and if we think we're going to play games and survive, we're kidding ourselves. This is dead serious."

For additional information on *Hage vs. United States*, or ways to get involved personally in the movement to restore American freedom and the fundamental principles upon which it is based, contact: Margaret Gabbard, Executive Director, Free Enterprise Legal Defense Fund, P.O. Box 44705, Boise, ID 83711, (208) 336-5922.

II. **States' Plans for Unappropriated Lands**

The National Biological Survey and the Wildlands Project (both described in Part Four, Chapter VI) are bold strokes toward achieving complete control of a nation through environmental regulation. One must only recall the creeping cancer precipitated by the Endangered Species Act to know these notions are not laughable. Bruce Babbitt and Dave Foreman are very serious about implementing their projects.

Dick Carver of Nye County, Nevada, is an equally serious man—a Nye County commissioner, in fact—who is not intimidated by the huff-and-blow of federal government and its musclemen in regulatory agencies. Carver believes most battles are won by taking the offensive, and he has formulated his own "bold stroke" to challenge both the past behavior and future intentions of the United States Government with respect to western lands.

It's called "The Nevada Plan."

Carver points out emphatically that the United States Constitution *does not* contain any authorization for the Federal Government of the United States to own, hold, or exert its dominion over any lands except whatever land it needs for its own governmental purpose as specified. Furthermore, the U.S. Government *is* authorized to acquire such needed land in any of the several states, by purchase, providing it shall be with the consent of the legislature of the state involved, and for those purposes specified. Carver cites Article 1, Section 8, Clause 17, of the U.S Constitution, to support his assertion.

He says, as far as Nye County is concerned, the Nevada state legislature granted through the prescribed process to the U.S. Government only the small tract of land occupied today by the Post Office in Tonopah. Further, the Nevada Revised Statutes clearly limit federal jurisdiction over the land in Nevada—so much so that NRS 321.5973 states: "*Subject to existing rights, all public lands in Nevada and all minerals not previously appropriated are the property of the State of Nevada and subject to its jurisdiction and control.*"

NRS 321.5973 continues: "*Until equivalent measures are enacted by the State of Nevada, the rights and privileges of the people of the State of Nevada under the National Forest Reserve Transfer Act . . . the General Mining Laws . . . the Homestead Act . . . the Taylor Grazing Act . . . the Carey Act . . . and the Public Rangelands Improvement Act . . . and all rights of way and easements for public utilities must be preserved under administration by the state.*"

Based on a thorough review of the Constitution, and of Nevada state statutes, Carver contends the U.S. Government neither owns nor controls any land within the boundaries of the state other than those acres purchased from or ceded by Nevada for military use and other specific functions of government. Ecosystem and wildlife management, and other preservationist programs, do not fall under that heading.

Carver says the framers of the Constitution—the founders of the United States of America—never intended for the Federal Government to be supreme, or that it would control large tracts of land in the individual states. He draws a chronology of important attitudes and events beginning with the original 13 colonies—where there was *no* "public domain." He writes: "When the 13 colonies became free *sovereign states*, all the land within the border of each state was either privately owned or belonged to that state. There was no central government, and each unit was a complete independent sovereign state, or small nation, unto itself. In the states that were created out of the Northwest Territory, lands not privately owned were called waste or unappropriated lands."

Judge Clel Georgetta wrote in his book *Golden Fleece in Nevada* that the Continental Congress adopted a resolution in 1780 requesting the 13 original states to surrender to the central government all the lands they claimed in the territory west of their original boundaries to the Mississippi, so the lands could be sold off to private interests to raise money to pay the Revolutionary War debt.

Georgetta wrote further: " . . . the independent sovereign states were first joined together in a Federal Union known as 'The Confederation' and in 1781 ratified 'The Articles of Confederation and Perpetual Union.' Those Articles contain the following words:

"Article II. Each state retains its sovereignty, freedom and independence, and every power, jurisdiction and right, which is not by this confederation expressly delegated to the United States in Congress assembled.

"Article IX. . . . provided also that no state shall be deprived of territory for the benefit of the United States."

Carver says there's no doubt that the purpose of such a guarantee was to "waylay" all fear in the individual states of joining the confederation. He emphasizes, "The framers of the Constitution of the United States were no more than statesmen representing the states. It was *not* federal people making the Constitution; it was *state* people making the Constitution. They gave *limited* powers to the federal government, and *retained* all other powers."

Carver goes on to explain provisions made legislatively by the Continental Congress in 1787 allowed the Federal Government to hold unsold western lands " . . . *in trust for the states that would be later created in the area."* The legislation stipulated that " . . . *whenever any of said states shall have sixty thousand inhabitants therein, such state shall be admitted . . . into the Congress of the United States, on equal footing with the original states, in all respects whatsoever . . . "*

Nowhere does Carver's argument break down.

As new states entered the Union, they were guaranteed by the original laws of the nation that all lands not privately owned within their boundaries belonged to them. The states were sovereign, and the states' citizens were sovereign. The Federal Government was born of them, with the people of the nation as the roots and foundation of it all. From the people grew the states, and from the states a nation was formed.

Even the "Supremacy Clause" of the Constitution guarantees merely that the states will not invade those areas specifically delegated to the Federal Government for the purposes of conducting government business—again, military reserves, post offices, federal buildings, et cetera.

Numerous other state statutes and constitutional provisions support Dick Carver's premise. Nowhere are these laws superseded by other statutes, federal authorization or court rulings. The federal bureaucracies have simply been allowed to swell up with self-importance over the decades to the point that they've gradually imposed themselves more and more onto the American public—mostly with the blessings of Congress and numerous administrations. The American people have "learned" to accept them as powerful agencies not to be reckoned with.

Dick Carver ain't buyin' it!

In late 1993, he sent a 26-page letter detailing and documenting his stand to Nevada Governor Bob Miller, Interior Secretary Bruce Babbitt, Agriculture Secretary Mike Espy, BLM Director Jim Baca, and acting Forest Service Chief David Unger. He sent copies to all Nevada legislators, all Nevada county commissioners and county attorneys, the Nevada Farm Bureau, the Cattlemans Association, Sheep Growers Association, Mining and Prospectors Associations, the Nevada Association of Cities, several U.S. senators and representatives, and dozens of BLM resource managers and Forest Service district rangers.

Supportive resolutions have been signed by all Nye County commissioners. "The Nevada Plan" has been picked up and endorsed by other counties and their commissioners across the state. Bureaucrats and environmental activists are watching this one with wary eyes. Bruce Babbitt was worried enough upon receipt of Carver's letter to travel to Nevada to try and appease the passion of this elected official with a love for the land and a conviction in his heart. He failed.

In early 1994, Carver activated a formal request for Babbitt and other federal agency heads to sit down with Nevada officials and officially relinquish their claims to millions of acres of so-called "federal lands" in the state of Nevada. If the desired result is not achieved, then Carver is prepared to lead the fight into the court system. If that occurs, he'll go with the full support of the Nevada Association of Counties and thousands of ranchers and miners and other unappropriated lands users, as well as state legislators, elected officials and property rights groups.

The Nevada Plan is breaking ground for similar challenges all across the country. Ed Presley, a Freedom of Information Act expert/investigator in Las Vegas, says, "The Nevada Plan, if it were in California, would be called the California Plan . . . in Utah, the Utah Plan . . . in Arizona, the Arizona Plan and so on."

Arizona Governor Fife Symington has taken an active role in defending and preserving states' rights, but from a slightly different perspective. At a major land use conference—held in Flagstaff in May of 1994—Symington outlined his vision for the management of "public" lands in Arizona. He called for the creation of a single new agency that would encompass the state Land Department, Arizona Game and Fish, as well as federal agencies like the Forest Service, the BLM and U.S. Fish and Wildlife Service. He stated simply that his idea would begin to "make some sense out of land policy" by eliminating overlapping jurisdictions that create problems and threaten the state's natural resources. Of course, a whole raft of opposition surfaced quickly from relentless environmentalists and defensive bureaucrats.

Carver says the key is to "activate," to get involved in the system and "do something." He says local governments must take an interest. "It's essential to get county commissioners behind you—or even better, leading the way." In some states they would be county supervisors. Ranchers and farmers, miners and loggers, property owners and property rights advocacy groups can get the ball rolling—preferably as a united group.

Numbers present might; the loudest voice is the one best heard. A groundswell of "States' Plans" would send Washington bureaucrats running for cover. Dick Carver believes the Nevada Plan is the shot that'll be heard across the nation.

For more information on ways to begin a "state plan" of your own, contact: Richard L. Carver, Vice Chairman, Nye County Board of Commissioners, HCR 60 Box 5400, Round Mountain, NV 89045-9801, (702) 377-2175.

III. The County Movement

If the absence of protest indicates an attitude of support, then a quiet majority of Americans can take responsibility for the regulations and governmental inequities imposed upon them. Often, however, a lack of public protest means little more than a lack of knowledge. Washington bureaucrats are very skilled at setting up restrictive regulatory policies before common citizens comprehend what is happening. Then, our _tolerant_ society, conditioned to _perceive_ the federal government as the supreme ruler of us all, accepts the new burden because "we can't do anything about it anyway."

(It's time for a wake-up call.)

Everyone is not being victimized. Regulations are imposed because they all—each and every one—benefit _somebody._ There is no other reason that accounts for 40,111 paid lobbyists working Capitol Hill in 1993. Lobbyists are paid to work for someone's special interests . . . and those interests usually translate to restrictions or regulations applying to someone else. The same year produced 93,000 pages of new rules in *The Federal Register*. These "rules" were written to apply to *you*!

Because of the investments in time, money and effort by those who stand to benefit, it is always more difficult to engage the wheels of regulation into reverse than it is to allow them to proceed forward. Some resolute defenders of local customs and cultures in Catron County, New Mexico, recognized this reality, and so began the "The County Movement."

Attorney-at-law Jeanette Burrage, Executive Director of the Northwest Legal Foundation, says, "In the absence of involvement at the county level in land use planning, federal agencies are not held accountable to local interests."

Activists of many inclinations are quick to fill the local void. Burrage points out aptly these "activists" usually do more harm than good because they know and care little about the local customs and cultures, and they bear none of the burden of local land use regulations. "The viable alternative of self-determination," writes Burrage, "exists at the county level of government."

Catron County, New Mexico, formulated, adopted and implemented the trailblazing blueprint for the County Government Movement. It includes some basic principles and philosophies, and six essential steps for implementation (those to follow). The primary premise for authorization of the plan is based on federal laws which *require* federal agencies to participate in "joint action" with county governments. Counties have *legal standing* to enter into such arrangements with federal agencies—*and* to preserve local customs and culture. But no one on the state or federal levels is going to force a county to behave in any such way because formal county management plans tend to get in the way of bureaucratic agendas.

Federal legislation supports the approach. Agencies of the Federal Government are required to preserve important cultural aspects of the national heritage under the National Environmental Policy Act—most often called NEPA.

Further, the Council for Environmental Quality (CEQ) requires federal agencies to " . . . _restore and enhance the quality of the human environment and avoid or minimize any possible adverse effects . . . upon the quality of the human environment . . ._ "

How could these basic protections have become so ignored and forgotten by the various agencies (FWS, CSC, BLM, NPS, et cetera) interpreting and enforcing their pet enactments (Clean Water Act, Endangered Species, Wild and Scenic Rivers)? Primarily, there are few county management plans in place to serve as protectors of citizens and shields from bureaucratic abuses.

Under CEQ regulations, federal agencies are directed to coordinate and conduct joint planning with local county governments. The jurisdiction and purposes of "joint planning" allow federal agencies to manage unappropriated lands for products and services to meet the needs of the nation, and at the same time allow county governments to protect the health and safety, economic welfare and the rights of their citizens—the county's customs, cultures, and economic stability _as defined by the people_ of the county. The county must also provide scientifically sound resource management recommendations and responsible alternatives for environmental protection and other considerations.

The process requires a great deal more diligence than simply stating, "We have a county plan." But the effort is rewarded by having locally elected and accountable officials participating in a "lead agency" jointly overseeing a comprehensive land use plan designed by the county's own citizens.

In formulating a "Comprehensive Land Use Plan," individual counties must closely adhere to six fundamental procedures. They are as follows:

Step I: Concerned Citizens
1. Form a Land Use Committee made up of citizens representing all industries, interests, and geographical areas in the county.
2. Submit a Redress of Grievance Petition to the County Government, requesting that the County Government initiate the process to develop a Comprehensive Land Use

Plan. The petition should request that the elements of the planning process be developed in the following order:

    A. Appointment of an authorized Land Planning Committee which will develop the plans and ordinances necessary to implement the plan.

    B. Adoption of an Interim Land Plan and an Environmental Protection Ordinance.

    C. Adoption of a Comprehensive Land Use Plan which defines the county's customs, cultures, and economy.

    D. Adoption of an ordinance to protect property rights (if not covered in the Comprehensive Plan).

    E. Adoption of an Ordinance to protect civil rights.

    F. Adoption of other ordinances applicable to the county.

    3. Submit with the petition a list of citizens to serve on the Land Use Committee, made up of representatives of all industries, interests, and geographical areas in the county.

Step II: County Government

    1. Authorize initiation of the process to develop a Comprehensive Land Use Plan for the county.

    2. Formally appoint a Land Planning Committee and give them responsibility to prepare all necessary documents for the plan.

Step III. Land Planning Committee

    1. Prepare an Interim Land Plan. This plan must fit the specific needs and requirements of the individual county. Each county must incorporate in their interim plan the policies that fit their specific situation.

    2. Prepare an Environmental Protection Ordinance. The purposes of this ordinance are to:

    A. Ensure the protection of the physical environment and the customs, cultures, and economic stability of the county.

    B. Require that federal agencies abide by NEPA and the CEQ regulations to conduct joint planning and environmental assessments with the county for proposed actions on federally claimed lands within the county.

C. Ensure full mitigation of adverse effects of environmental decisions to county and its citizens.

D. Provide policies and procedures for the county to develop environmental impact statements and environmental assessments on their own if necessary.

Step IV. County Government

1. Adopt the Interim Land Plan and the Environmental Protection Ordinances.

2. Notify the appropriate federal agencies that the county: one, is operating under an Interim Land Plan and an Environmental Protection Ordinance; and, two, is developing a Comprehensive Land Use Plan. The notification should include the name of the point of contact in the county and a request that the agencies provide the county with early notification of all planning and implementation actions.

Step V. Land Planning Committee

1. Prepare a Comprehensive Land Use Plan. The purposes are to:

A. Document the county's customs and cultures that must be preserved under NEPA. These must be defined only by county residents through public meetings, personal interviews and surveys.

B. Define the county's economic structure, using the expertise and resources of state and university economists.

C. Define the desired land use objectives which will preserve the county's culture, customs and economic stability.

D. Give the County Government the ability to "coordinate" with federal agencies pursuant to NEPA, as well as participating agency regulations.

E. Provide the opportunity for the county to describe property rights recognized under local law and custom within the county. (The U.S. Supreme Court has determined "property rights" can only be defined on a local level. Therefore, the County Government can use the Comprehensive Plan to define and document property rights to be protected by the U.S. Constitution.)

F. Define the organization and basic procedures for the operation of the land planning committees (formed according to the individual county's various industries and economic structure) which will be responsible for implementation of the plan.

2. Prepare an ordinance that repeals the Interim Land Plan.

3. Prepare a Civil Rights Ordinance. Note that civil rights include protection for all constitutionally guaranteed rights, including but not limited to property rights.

4. Prepare a Property Rights Ordinance (if no definition of property rights appears in the Comprehensive Plan). This should be based on Presidential Executive Order 12630.

5. Prepare any other ordinances applicable to the county.

Step VI. County Government

1. Appoint land planning committees for individual functional areas to operate under the Land Planning Committee. These committees become involved in joint planning activities with the various federal agencies. (The chairmen of these committees make up the Land Planning Committee.)

2. Hire natural resource management specialists in the major land use discipline(s) needed for the county (range conservationist, wildlife biologist, mining engineer, et cetera).

3. Notify the respective federal agencies that the county has adopted its Comprehensive Land Use Plan and provide names of the points of contact for each committee, as well as the resource specialist(s).

4. Enter into Memorandums of Understanding (MOU) for joint planning with all applicable federal agencies.

The Catron County approach to comprehensive land use management by the respective governments of counties provides a comparison of benefits when federal agencies are monitored by county governments as opposed to special interest activists. Initially, while county governments are made up of elected representatives of the people, the eco-activists represent only the interests of their own groups. County governments foster a concern for proper use and management of the land for the people in the county, based on customs and cultures and economic stability, when preservationist groups singlemindedly fail to consider (and are seldom affected by) socioeconomic ramifications of their interests. Local counties serve as watchdogs and provide valuable assistance and support to federal agencies, while outside interests encourage mismanagement of valuable resources and hamper wise planning efforts.

The basic principles upon which the County Government Movement is based include regulatory integrity, abidance with the law, the separation of powers, limiting the persuasion of federal government, the ability to self-govern, the guarantee of property and other basic civil rights.

As an effective example, four of eight counties in Nebraska implemented land use plans to deal with a Wild and Scenic Rivers designation on the Niobrara River. Those four counties now have active roles in the management of streamside areas, while the four counties without plans have been seriously impacted by federal regulations.

Officials in Catron County admit their plan is the result of a "grassroots response to an ever-growing federal bureaucracy which has strayed well beyond, and even violates, the provisions of the Constitution established by our founding fathers." They take encouragement from the knowledge that supporters of the County Government Movement are proud Americans who love the land and desire a long-term relationship with it through the existence of inalienable rights.

Just as with the Nevada Plan being equally effective in Arizona, Utah and other states, the Catron County Plan would apply just as soundly to Yuma County, Arizona . . . Shasta County, California or Linn County, Oregon. As the word spreads and concerned citizens begin to recognize the unique protective value in this approach, numerous comprehensive land use plans are being structured in individual counties from Alaska to Arizona.

To obtain a detailed guide on initiating a comprehensive land use plan in any county anywhere, contact: Howard Hutchinson, Legal Researcher, Coalition of Arizona/New Mexico Counties, P.O. Box 125, Glenwood, NM 88039-0125 (505) 539-2709 . . .

Or: Danny Fryar, County Administrator, Catron County Government, Reserve, NM 87830, (505) 533-6423.

IV. The Importance of Private Property

When identifying the key principles necessary to maintaining a free society, the framers of the U.S. Constitution cited the ownership of property as the most essential element. The freedom and right to own land was the most basic of all fundamental civil liberties. This is the same freedom and right that many radical preservationists and some powerful bureaucrats would have us surrender or perceive in some modified form.

(Bruce Babbitt called it a "communitarian interpretation" before adding, "You can't build fences around property." I know a nation of landowners who disagree.)

At the 72nd Annual Meeting of the Arizona Farm Bureau in late 1993, Arizona Governor Fife Symington said, "To say that property is the cornerstone of liberty comes up short. I would say that property *is* liberty. You start fooling around with private property rights and you are on the road to slavery. The only thing left with any power at all would be a large central government."

The authors of the Constitution said it most succinctly: "*Either you have the right to own property, or you are the property of a totalitarian government.*"

A primary premise of democratic government is that private citizens should earn and own the wealth of a nation.

This is not possible when the government owns or controls the resource base. It seems illogical, then, that by early 1994 the U.S. Government controlled somewhere between one-third and one-half of all the land in the country, and millions of taxpayer dollars are being used every year for stepped-up acquisitions.

Another misconception of the bureaucrats is that government can best manage the lands and resources for the people. This is a ruse. Big government has never managed _anything_ effectively. The motivation to control inspires the agency bureaucrats to acquire more . . . and, of course, there's a self-preservationist attitude at work here. Government is the biggest employer in the U.S.; there is no other sector of business or industry with as many hundreds of thousands of employees, each finding ways to demonstrate his worth and hold onto his job.

The plain fact of the matter is: private ownership of land is the most effective system of resource management. The depleted resources of eastern Europe, where totalitarian governments exercised control for tens of decades, demonstrates this well. It's estimated that another 100 years are needed for private initiative to restore the lands, lakes, rivers and forests there. Further, when the first explorers came to California (where no government existed), they ate their horses, and sometimes one another, in order to survive because the land was barren. Early settlers used their knowledge to create water sources and meadows, ranches and farms. Vegetation and wildlife flourished in concert with livestock and private land management. Government had nothing to do with it.

Since the mid-1950s, government has taken an ever tighter stranglehold on American resources and private land management. Predator control has become restricted. Wetlands and endangered species protection have rendered much land useless. More and more costly regulations have been imposed, making effective management by landowners increasingly more difficult.

Property owners are beginning to fight back, but mostly in clusters. If a particular area is affected by an endangered species, national park enlargement or agency regulation, then landowners become activists. Vast numbers still uninformed or unaffected remain complacent. Federal bureaucracies and environmental groups recognize this fact as perhaps their last opportunity to mount a victorious offensive. They are quickly preparing their strategies. The Wilderness Society has compiled a 300-page status report on the "Wise-Use Movement" across the 50 states, detailing areas of strength and vulnerability among property owners.

(Then President of the Society George Frampton is now Assistant Director of the Interior Department—first lieutenant to Secretary Babbitt. See how closely it's all tied together?)

The report identifies wise-use/property rights initiatives, and labels the movement as "grassroots." This is particularly frightening to the opposition. As stated by Debra Callahan of the W. Alton Jones Foundation, "The minute the wise-use people capture that high ground (recognition as true stewards of the land), we almost have not got a winning message left in our quiver."

Another disturbing aspect of wise use, as seen by federal and environmental power mongers, is stated perceptively by National Wildlife Federation attorney Glen Sugameli: "They aren't doing this to get compensation for taking property. They are doing this to stop regulation."

Property rights advocates agree wholeheartedly.

It's contradictory to assert that owning property is the most basic of all principles of freedom, then restrict the use of that property through governmental regulation. More and more property owners and land users are conveying this sentiment to their Washington representatives, and a case was clearly made during the 1993 debate over the National Biological Survey. An amendment prohibiting entry onto private property without written landowner consent drew such support from Democrats and Republicans alike that the bill's sponsor, Rep. Gerry Studds of Massachusetts, said reauthorizations of Clean Water and Endangered Species had better include property rights wording because " . . . we almost had a riot on the floor of the House last week."

There's a resounding unspoken message in Studds' reaction, if landowners will only hear it and respond. At a time when President Clinton is considering scrapping the Takings Executive Order of 1988, he might as well have said, "Now is the time to strengthen congressional support for property rights by putting additional pressure on your legislators."

There is might in numbers. State and federal lawmakers listen to the loudest voices—whether its the special interests or those fighting for basic American fundamentals. Conversely, silent voices are never heard. Neither do they carry an impact, no matter their numbers.

Examples on the local level might include the rallying by Ann Corcoran and Alice Menks against National Park Service encroachment. When numbers swelled, the agency began to reevaluate. Similar action was taken by Peggy Reigle of Dorchester County, Maryland, when broadened wetlands delineation allowed her entire 118-acre farm to be classified. The land had never been wet, and suddenly the prospects for a housing development planned by the Reigles as a retirement project seemed lost. Reigle started the Fairness to Land Owners Committee to assist themselves and other landowners facing devastating governmental regulation. Her effort spread across 38 states, attracting more than 11,000 members.

Congress listens to those kinds of voices.

The private property movement has given birth to the Alliance For America—an umbrella group encompassing 500 member organizations and thousands of individuals with property rights concerns. The Alliance acts as a diligent watchdog, supplying information on pending legislation and issues affecting property rights, as well as ways of combating bureaucratic regulation.

Cattlemen, farmers, loggers and miners, developers and homeowners are learning it's smart to become a "joiner." Groups supporting the basic American Dream exist in every state across the nation, as do coalitions of such groups. Every new member makes their voices stronger and louder.

(That's how the environmentalists did it, folks. Only, there's a much clearer picture within wise-use/property rights organizations as to what the full memberships actually represent. A majority of the members of Sierra Club _don't know_ what their membership dollars and contributions are used for.)

People for the West! is a grassroots group gaining a lot of respect and political notice. At the end of 1993, more than 100 local chapters were in active operation from California to Missouri, from Alaska to Texas. The rapidly expanding organization is dedicated to protecting customs and cultures, property rights and wise-use practices for all freedom-loving Americans. One enormous property rights group recognized nationwide is the American Farm Bureau Federation, which maintains an active lobby is Washington. Additionally, State Farm Bureau Federations provide inspiration and guidance to county chapters all across the country. They are easily accessible, membership is inexpensive, and members are not required to be farmers—or even landowners. They just need to support the rights and freedoms guaranteed Americans by the U.S. Constitution.

Anyone wanting to become very quickly involved in the protection of private property rights, and the wise use of federally controlled lands, should look in their local phone directories for Farm Bureau Insurance Services, or Farm Bureau offices listed according to state or county names. Otherwise, write: Dean Kleckner, President, American Farm Bureau Federation, 225 Touhy Avenue, Park Ridge, IL 60068, (312) 399-5700.

Freedom-loving Americans must band together so their concerns are voiced in numbers and taken seriously by those elected to represent them. Short of a responsive congressional ear, the last salvation of American rights and freedoms will come through costly litigation—if at all. Radical preservationists, greedy bureaucrats and jaded politicians do not constitute a majority when stacked against the millions of Americans who still believe in America. The silent majority only lacks organization.

The following are a few more ways to remedy the imbalance:

Oregon Lands Coalition, 280 Court Street NE., Suite 5, Salem, OR 97301, (503) 342-4814

Blue Ribbon Coalition, P.O. Box 5449, Pocatello, ID 83202, (208) 237-1557

Western States Public Lands Coalition (People For the West!), P.O. 4345, Pueblo, CO 81003, (719) 543-9473

Range, P.O. Box 639, Carson City, NV 89702-0639, (702) 882-0121

Abundant Wildlife Society of North America, 12665 Hwy 59 N., Gillette, WY 82716 (307) 682-2826

21st Century Science & Technology, P.O. Box 16285, Washington, DC 20041 (703) 777-7473

National Inholders Association, 30218 NE 82nd Avenue, P.O. Box 400, Battle Ground, WA 98604, (206) 687-3087

Land Rights Letter, P.O. Box 568, Sharpsburg, MD 21782, (518) 725-8835

Endangered Species Coordinating Council, P.O. Box 33273, Washington, DC 20033-0273, (202) 463-2779

Alliance For America, P.O. Box 449, Caroga Lake, NY 12032, (518) 835-6702

Center for the Defense of Free Enterprise, 12500 NE Tenth Place, Bellevue, WA 98005, (206) 455-5038

V. **Welcome to the World of Politics**

A widespread organized armed uprising against an oppressive U.S. Government is not likely. If such a revolution were to occur, it would be the bloodiest conflict this nation has ever seen. Our idled armed forces would move in masses to put down the insurrection. A confused and terrified Commander-in-Chief would order his war-hungry generals to restore civil obedience, and millions of Americans would die.

It won't happen . . . because we are *civilized* and *tolerant* . . . and we *perceive* our government to be more powerful than it is. Beyond that, it won't happen because it's not necessary.

Our democratic system of government is still the best form of government in the world. That's why so many good and decent Americans are rallying to preserve the cornerstones laid by the founding fathers of the nation. Land rights crusader Ed Presley reiterates, "The Constitution is a living document. It is alive and well. Contrary to what you hear . . . the law system that we have is the finest in the world."

Americans—without rising up in arms against their nation's government—wield the most powerful political persuader known to mankind. Granted by the Constitution, the *individual vote* is intact, and the right to exercise it is *not* being threatened. The American public must stop taking it for granted. Groups and individuals who want their voices heard in the lawmaking process should work to inform others through the media, public service announcements, radio and television talk shows, newspaper editorials, letters to editors, rallies, mailings, newsletters, local chambers of commerce, telephone campaigns and other means of promoting public awareness.

Numbers mean might, and educating local communities and neighborhoods will generate numbers.

There's an attitude in America that needs changing, however, before any major adjustments are achieved in the political shuffle. It all has to do, again, with how the so-called "powerful politicians" are *perceived*. All too often, when a U.S senator or congressman graces a gathering of constituents, the voting public (the ones with the *real* power) scrape and bow, and kiss the hands they've elected to serve them, hoping to gain small morsels of political favor like beggars cadging handouts.

This is backwards!

Washington politicians should come humbly begging their constituents for acceptance and approval, and asking what their political pleasure is. Career politicians do not make for healthy government, and neither do dishonest ones. Oftentimes, one leads to the other, but American voters continue to reelect incumbents—no matter what they've done. That's not the incumbents' fault. It's the *voters'* fault, and the system will continue to display most of its flaws as long as we allow it.

Voters have got to make elected officials *fear* their voting strength. Politicians must know that when they cast a vote that's not representative of their constituents' sentiments, it will cost them their job. Perks and personal favors from special interest lobbyists should not get them reelected. A performance on Capitol Hill—one vote at a time—satisfactory to the constituency back home is all that should matter.

The scenario is not outside the realm of possibility. Again, public awareness campaigns and mounting those numbers are the key elements of success. The same holds true when supporting or opposing specific pieces of legislation. Keeping informed is first and foremost, whether it be through membership in political action groups or subscribing to newsletters. Laws passed in the Congress of the United States are not emblazoned on stone tablets by shooting bolts of lightning. Laws can be revised—even repealed, although the latter is not common. Prohibition and 55-mph speed limit, however, are two examples of unpopular legislation that got reworked to suit public sentiment.

The Clean Water Act needs to be fixed to alleviate thousands of injustices pertaining to arbitrary wetlands designations. The Endangered Species Act is now criticized even by biologists and other members of the scientific community. In all fairness to members of Congress, these laws were enacted with good intentions. Experience has pointed up the desperate need for legislative repair in both instances. Public outcry—*louder than preservationist whining*—can make it happen.

Anyone who feels "someone else will take care of it" is a weak link in the chain. Too many weak links cause the chain to break, and that can be as fatal to an effort as severing an umbilical cord to an unborn child. Americans must stand together or continue to see their basic rights and freedoms slip away.

Another way to make politics work for you is to become a politician. Don't discard this approach too quickly. Dick Carver is a home-grown grassroots politician in Nye County, Nevada, and he and his Nevada Plan have caused some heads in Washington to turn rather abruptly. Now, while Carver may be the exception, he *could* be the rule.

Bill Grannell, Executive Director of Western States Public Lands Coalition, writes: "Getting involved in a political party and getting your voice heard is neither tough nor complicated. But, it does take patience and persistence. These are lessons the Green Movement learned years ago, and today it's paying off big." Grannell adds, " . . . you can believe that no one has a lock on America's political process."

Of utmost importance is party affiliation—not necessarily which party, but the fact that party affiliation exists. The prospective politician must consider numerous factors when choosing a party—which party is in power, personal political philosophies, local political vacancies and opportunities, the means for getting involved as early in the process as possible. Registered Independents usually can't vote in primaries or participate in caucuses, so this would be a consideration.

Grannell says few politicians surface with revolutionary political ideas. They instead serve as mouthpieces for ideas brought forth through "the arcane and little understood process of political party platforms." These ideas are assembled initially by the "rank-and-file" party people.

(*That*, my friends, is where *you* should be, because that's where the environmental activists are!)

"Party platforms" begin at the county level. Any party member—*anyone*—can have a voice or submit a political idea. These "ideas" are often the bases for new laws, even at the national level. The contributor of an idea at the county level should submit a formal resolution to the central party committee or caucus, stating the intents and purposes of the proposal. A collection of local resolutions is then molded into a statement of party principles—a "platform."

The county platform is forwarded to the state party for consideration. The policies that survive (and many of them do) are sent on to the national party conventions. A national platform is written, and the separate issues comprising the platform are known as "planks." Planks provide the "meat" for effective speeches by national politicians striving to please the voters back home.

A helpful rung up on the political ladder is the elected position of precinct committee person. The various states regulate the procedure for getting there differently, but none of them is difficult. In some states you can nominate yourself. In others, you may have to gather a few signatures on a nominating petition. The county clerk's office at the local courthouse will have all the requirements, and the paperwork. They'll even help you with it.

If there's competition for the position, you may have to campaign, but on a precinct basis that usually involves little more than calling on your neighbors and asking for their votes. County clerks also have lists of registered voters that are beneficial at this time. Many "wannabe" politicians set their sights over and beyond the precinct committees, leaving them more readily available to the novice who really is serious about making a difference.

Election of precinct representatives occurs during the primary, or at a party caucus, depending in the process in your state. Once elected, you'll be asked to serve on committees and become more active in the political process within your county. And you'll be in a position to apply your own voice to the shaping of your party principles—your _political platform_.

There's no restriction on how politically active (or effective) you might want to become. First, precinct person, then committee chairman . . . perhaps city councilman, county commissioner or state representative. Who knows?

The facts of the matter are: The louder you speak, the better you are heard . . . and a groundswell of loud voices can change the direction of a nation.

VI. **Light at the End of the Tunnel**

There's hope!

Federal Judge Harold Ryan ruled at the end of 1993 that the Bruneau hot springs snail had been improperly listed as endangered. The lives and livelihoods of some 59 farm and ranch families in southwestern Idaho's Bruneau Valley were seriously affected by the listing of the microscopic underground mollusk. After a concerted fight by Owyhee County officials and residents, the Farm Bureau and Idaho Cattlemen's Association, Judge Ryan invalidated the listing— the first delisting of a species in the history of the Endangered Species Act.

This was a milestone.

Judge Ryan ruled that specific listing procedures were violated during the snail's listing process—as has been the case in hundreds of other listings. He stated unequivocally that the Federal Government is not above the law—something that needs stressing far more often than it is. It was shown that faulty scientific data was largely responsible for the snail's listing—another common occurrence. These aspects of the case should serve as precedents in future courtrooms, and should certainly be acknowledged by Congress in any modification of the ESA.

Other crusades and crusaders have made progress.

Some access to private cemeteries has been restored to the families removed from their homes and properties along the National Buffalo River in northern Arkansas, thanks to the continuing efforts of local crusader Little Leon Somerville.

Marion Palmer, a farmer in Modoc County, California, won a landmark first-round court battle against the Oregon Natural Resources Council in September of 1993. ONRC eco-radicals Andy Kerr and Wendell Wood were named as defendants in a lawsuit that charged misuse of the endangered status of sucker fish to restrict irrigation water on Palmer's farm. Palmer claimed in court the ONRC used the short-nosed and Lost River suckers as surrogates "to mount a fund-raising campaign for their own gain." He tallied his losses in crop production and property value at $40,000. ONRC lawyers sought dismissal of the case on grounds that it had no merit. Judge Guy Martin ruled otherwise.

On the other side of the country, conservation groups had their eyes and hearts set on a Wild and Scenic designation for the Pemigewasset River in New Hampshire. Corporate foundation monies were secured to push the project forward. Paid organizers worked individual local communities. Area residents were bombarded with mailings and telephone campaigns urging support of the project. Proponents of Wild and Scenic designation spent upwards of $50,000 in a few short months.

Meanwhile, the New Hampshire Landowners Alliance worked to educate the public with hard facts about other Wild and Scenic designations. They organized rallies and meetings and public forums. They wrote letters to local papers and brought in speakers from around the country to share their experiences with the National Park Service. They waged a media campaign. Their total budget was $3,000, but they stirred enough opposition that the NPS agreed to relax their push for designation in areas where towns voted it down. In March of 1993, six of seven communities said "NO," and the NPS backed off.

In June of 1991, a small group of independent logging companies—based mostly around the tiny timber-dependent community of Sweet Home, Oregon—filed suit in U.S. District Court for the District of Columbia, challenging the "excessive" guidelines for protecting the northern spotted owl. It seems the word "harm," with respect to the protected owl, was being interpreted by the Fish and Wildlife Service to include private actions on private land anywhere within a 3,960-acre circle around every owl's nest. Most of the plaintiffs in this suit were operators of small family-owned companies dependent on private timber sales to survive. Due to over-zealous protection of a species known to nest anywhere from third-growth forest to the insides of a broken Circle-K sign, these companies were faced with laying off employees, defaulting on insurance coverage and losing their entire operations for their inability to make payments on operating loans and taxes.

After nearly three years of continuous effort through court motions and arguments, advisements, filings, rulings, appeals and all the other legal ploys known only to lawyers, a three-judge panel on the U.S Court of Appeals reached a two-to-one decision in March of 1994. The ruling in *Sweet Home vs. Babbitt* determined the "harm" regulation unlawful in that it effectively transformed ordinary private land use actions—like harvesting private trees—into prohibited ESA "takings."

In short, the Court found that Congress had never authorized such a regulation. However, that didn't stop FWS from interpreting and *enforcing* it that way. It took a long and costly legal battle to loosen the first finger of a double-fisted death-grip around the throats of Northwestern industry and property owners. Assistant Secretary of the Interior George Frampton (a man who does not believe in either free enterprise or private property rights) immediately promised to appeal to the U.S. Supreme Court. Nonetheless, a meaningful victory was achieved . . . a point was made . . . a message sent. Another voice was heard.

The battles are many, the battlefields nationwide. But every tiny victory is a candle in the cavern providing light to the end of the tunnel. While grassroots efforts to save and protect property rights and wise-use practices are causing left-wing bureaucrats and eco-salvationists to take notice, the movement is hardly enough to stem the flow of assaults coming from radical visionaries, noetic earth-worshipers, wealthy preservationist groups, socialist bureaucrats and out-of-touch politicians.

The battle over property rights and other basic civil liberties is not being fought in a dark and endless tunnel. There's light up ahead. It's coming in the form of an awakening American public. The crusaders are making some noise, and their ranks are filling with enthusiastic supporters.

The generals leading the troops are men and women like Nevada rancher Wayne Hage and his attorneys Mark Pollot and Thomas Hookano of San Francisco; like Ann Corcoran of Sharpsburg, Maryland, and Alice Menks of

Graves Mill, Virginia; William Perry Pendley of the Mountain States Legal Foundation in Denver; Clark County, Nevada, rancher Clivon Bundy and Freedom of Information Act investigator Ed Presley of Las Vegas; Ron Arnold of the Center for the Defense of Free Enterprise in Bellevue, Washington; Howard Hutchinson of the Coalition of Arizona/New Mexico Counties in Glenwood, New Mexico; Little Leon Somerville of Cozahome, Arkansas; Jeanette Burrage of the Northwest Legal Foundation in Seattle; Commissioner Dick Carver of Nye County, Nevada; Bill Grannell of Western States Public Lands Coalition in Pueblo, Colorado; Don Sanborn of Lakeview, Oregon; Governor Fife Symington of Arizona.

There are so many more. Each one needs help—a lot of help.

Your help.

Every community has dedicated, sound-thinking individuals who might lead a local property rights cause, start a new chapter of People for the West!, begin publishing a newsletter, investigate the source and content of environmental curriculum at local schools. The national groups and coalitions need to know of these people and their numbers of supporters. There's a lot of help available, and it becomes a reciprocal thing; everyone is stronger for the relationship.

The United States Constitution and its Bill of Rights guaranteed an opportunity to all Americans—the right to own a piece of the nation, to live as free men and women, to pursue their happiness and destinies by molding and shaping their own American Dreams. These ideals are still very much alive, and a new appreciation of fundamental American freedoms is welling in the hearts of millions.

Elements needed to solidify the New American Spirit are involvement, unity, awareness and perseverance.

All freedom-loving Americans must get involved because—remember—_it's the loudest voice that gets heard!_ A clear understanding of the battle being fought—whether it's a local concern or a national issue—is imperative to waging an intelligent and effective offensive. That's right—_offensive._ As previously pointed out, _battles are not won from a defensive position!_

President Calvin Coolidge said all there is to be said about perseverance: "Nothing in this world can take the place of persistence. Talent will not; nothing is more common than unsuccessful people with talent. Genius will not; unrewarded genius is almost a proverb. Education will not; the world is full of educated derelicts. Persistence and determination alone are omnipotent."

The anti-property rights/pro-environmental movement recognized, learned and adopted this philosophy about two decades before anyone else realized their fundamental freedoms were eroding. Therefore, the preservationist movement scored some early crippling victories, but the battle is far from over. Property owners and millions more who still believe in the American Dream are becoming "preservationists" in their own right as they mount a united front for the preservation of our founding fathers' convictions . . . the Constitution and Bill of Rights . . . the ownership and use of land . . . for basic inalienable civil rights . . .

. . . for the preservation of the United States of America.

THE END

Editor's Note to Mainstream America:

To help save the American Dream, with the aid of this book and its author, write: *Rawhide Western Publishing, PO Box 327, Safford, Arizona 85548,* or call toll-free 1-800-428-5956. To become a vital link in the information chain, use the convenient order form inside the back cover of this book. Multiple orders will receive the largest possible discount. Books can be sold at retail as an effective fundraiser for your group.

Speaking engagements with the author can be arranged through the above-named agency—same address, same number. We're all in the battle. Together, we can make a difference.

BIBLIOGRAPHY

Chappell, Jack Wayne, *The Wilderness Rape* (Winona, MN; The New West House, 1985)

Chase, Alston, *Playing God in Yellowstone: The Destruction of America's First National Park* (New York, NY; Harcourt Brace Jovanovich, 1986)

Hage, Wayne, *Storm Over Rangelands: Private Rights in Federal Lands* (Bellevue, WA; Free Enterprise Press, 1989)

Hill, Karen and Piccirelli, Annette, *Gale Environmental Sourcebook* (Detroit, MI; Gale Research, Inc., 1992)

Pollot, Mark L., *Grand Theft and Petit Larceny: Property Rights in America* (San Francisco, CA; Pacific Research Institute for Public Policy, 1993)

Wilkinson, Charles F., *The American West: A Narrative Bibliography* (Niwot, CO; University Press of Colorado, 1989)

Bailey, Ronald, "The Eco-Crisis Myth", *The American Legion*, October, 1993

Fitzgerald, Randy, "When a Law Goes Haywire", *Reader's Digest*, September, 1993

Pennisi, Elizabeth, "Conservation's Ecocentrics", *Science News*, September 11, 1993

Gardner, Cliff, "Wetlands Management in Today's Environment" (Stewards of the Range video)

Menks, Alice and Thomas, Leri, "Us vs. NPS" (Virginians For Property Rights/Madison County Preservation Coalition report on National Park Service, 1992)

Abundant Wildlife, January/February 1993; March/April 1993

Arkansas Democrat Gazette, June 30, 1993; July 11, 1993

Arkansas Times, December 1988

Arizona Farm Bureau News, October 1993; November 1993

Capital Press, January 24, 1992; March 6, 1992; March 19,1993

Delta Farm Press, June 25, 1993

Farm Bureau News, August 16, 1993

Focus: Delaware/New Jersey Edition, October 1993

Forbes, January 22, 1990

Herald and News (Klamath Falls, OR), July 12, 1990; August 7, 1990; November 25, 1991; June 14, 1992; December 21, 1992; January 24, 1993; January 27, 1993; July 11, 1993; November 17, 1993

Land Rights Letter, July/August 1993; September 1993; October 1993; November 1993

Newsweek, April 25, 1993

Oregon Business, August 1989

Oregonian (Portland, OR), February 1993; October 29, 1993

People for the West! September 1993; October 1993; November 1993; December 1993; January 1994

Range Magazine, Summer 1992

Stewards of the Range, May 1992; September 1992; January 1993; July 1993; October 1993; November 1993

Wall Street Journal, January 11, 1990

Washington Times, December 14, 1991

. . . and dozens more, ranging from personal letters to the Constitution of the United States. Between the two came newsletters and memos, governmental agency documents, memorandums of understanding, congressional legislation, environmental impact statements, regional newspapers too many to mention, hundreds of documented personal case histories, and a 292-page wild-eyed analysis of the "Wise Use Movement," prepared under direction of then Wilderness Society President George Frampton (now Assistant Director of the Interior Department), with detailed strategies on how to stamp out property rights and take over the entire country on a state-by-state basis.

No freeman shall be taken,
imprisoned, or disseized, or outlawed,
or exiled, or in any way harmed . . .
save by the lawful judgment of his peers
or by the law of the land.

Magna Carta, 1215

INDEX

No man of what estate or condition
that he be, should be put out of his lands
or tenements, nor taken, nor imprisoned,
nor disherited . . .
without being brought to answer
by due process of law.

Petition of Right, 1628

*No person [shall be] deprived of life,
liberty, or property, without due process
of law; nor shall private property be
taken for public purpose, without
just compensation.*

Amendment V, U.S. Constitution, 1787

SEE
REVERSE SIDE
FOR
MAXIMUM
SAVINGS!

Discount Order Form

Every American who has ever pledged allegiance to the United States' flag . . . has ever benefited from the existence of the U.S. Constitution . . . has ever believed in the American Dream . . . should know about the spreading threat of runaway environmentalism, the loss of inalienable rights, and the push for centralized government control.

YOU CAN HELP SPREAD THE WORD!

For additional copies of *Surviving the Second Civil War: The Land Rights Battle . . . and How To Win It*:

Send this form for discounts (check line below)

_____1 copy @ $12.95 + $2.00 ship/handle = $14.95
_____2 copies @ $11.65 ea. + ship/handle = $26.30
_____3 copies @ $11.01 ea. + ship/handle = $37.53
_____5 copies @ $9.71 ea. + ship/handle = $56.05
_____10/more @ $7.78 ea. + $1.25 ea. s/h = $_____
_____20/more @ $7.50 ea. + $1.00 ea. s/h = $_____

SAVE 40%+ ON ORDERS OF 10 OR MORE.
Please remit payment with order to: Rawhide Western Publishing, PO Box 327, Safford, AZ 85548.
  Allow 3 weeks for delivery.   COD orders welcome.

Call toll-free: 1-800-428-5956 (for orders only)
Office phone: 602-428-5956 (more information)
Fax line: 602-428-7010 (for fast COD shipping)